lonely planet KIDS

A KID'S GUIDE TO

NEW YORK CITY

LET THE ADVENTURE BEGIN!

by Alexa Ward

Project Editor: Priyanka Lamichhane
Designers: John Foster, Andrew Mansfield
Publishing Director: Piers Pickard
Publisher: Rebecca Hunt
Art Director: Emily Dubin
Print Production: Nigel Longuet

The Lonely Planet Kids Travel Guides series is produced in partnership
with the WonderLab Group, LLC.

Special thanks to our city consultant, Abigail Blasi,
and editor, Rose Davidson.

Published in May 2025 by Lonely Planet Global Limited
CRN: 554153
ISBN: 9781837585243
www.lonelyplanet.com/kids
© Lonely Planet 2025
10 9 8 7 6 5 4 3 2 1
Printed in Malaysia

STAY IN TOUCH
lonelyplanet.com/contact

Lonely Planet Office:
IRELAND
Digital Depot, Roe Lane (off Thomas St),
Digital Hub, Dublin 8, D08 TCV4, Ireland

MIX
Paper | Supporting
responsible forestry
FSC™ C021741

Paper in this book is certified against the
Forest Stewardship Council™ standards.
FSC™ promotes environmentally responsible,
socially beneficial and economically viable
management of the world's forests.

A KID'S GUIDE TO

NEW YORK CITY

LET THE ADVENTURE BEGIN!

by Alexa Ward

CONTENTS

IMAGE: A bird's-eye view of Manhattan.

HOW TO USE THIS BOOK

Are you in search of a city's most delish desserts or wild about urban wilderness? Maybe you want to check out some places to play or discover the history and mysteries of the city. Or, perhaps, all of the above? Each chapter of this book has a unique theme. You can read the book from beginning to end or dip in and out! Don't forget to scour each page for fun facts, places, people, and more. Here are some highlighted features in the book.

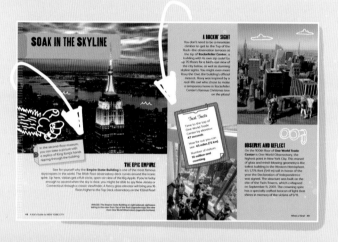

Like collecting facts and stats?

Check these out.

NYC is another way to say New York City.

What makes this city tick?

Look for "Heading to Broadway" on pages 70-81 or "Kaleidoscope of Culture" on pages 82-93.

Curious about the weirdest, wackiest, and most unheard-of spots?

"Secrets of the City" is on pages 118-129.

Need something to do while waiting for the train, bus, plane, or car?

Look for "What's the Difference?" on pages 130-133.

WELCOME TO NEW YORK CITY!

Picture this: skyscrapers that seem to touch the clouds, streets buzzing with excitement, and a city that never sleeps! It's New York City, a place full of awesome adventures! In the middle of Times Square, gigantic billboards light up the streets like fireworks. At the iconic Empire State Building, incredible views let you see far and wide. On the water, the Statue of Liberty stands tall over New York Harbor. And sprawling Central Park is a perfect place to play. But this guide isn't just about the usual stuff—it's packed with exciting facts, cool stats, and information that will leave you in awe. Let's go!

HELLO

IMAGE: The Statue of Liberty overlooking NYC.

FOOD FUN

Hungry for a snack or delicious treat? In NYC you can find food from almost every place on Earth. Try West African fufu, Polish pierogis, Japanese sashimi, and Puerto Rican tostones, or grab some fresh local produce from one of the city's many farmers markets. After all, this *is* the Big Apple!

MAPPING IT OUT

There is so much to see in NYC! Check out this map, highlighting some popular spots found in this book.

NEW YORK BOTANICAL GARDEN

BRONX ZOO

YANKEE STADIUM

MANHATTAN

HUDSON RIVER

CENTRAL PARK

METROPOLITAN MUSEUM OF ART

ROOSEVELT ISLAND

TIMES SQUARE BROADWAY

EMPIRE STATE BUILDING

FLATIRON BUILDING

CHELSEA

SOHO

EAST RIVER

EAST VILLAGE

NEW JERSEY

FINANCIAL DISTRICT

BROOKLYN BRIDGE

WILLIAMSBURG

BARCLAYS CENTER

STATUE OF LIBERTY

BROOKLYN MUSEUM

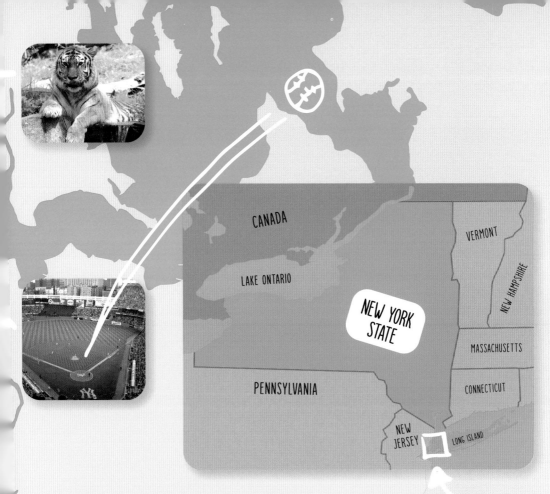

CANADA

VERMONT

NEW HAMPSHIRE

LAKE ONTARIO

NEW YORK STATE

MASSACHUSETTS

PENNSYLVANIA

CONNECTICUT

NEW JERSEY

LONG ISLAND

New York City

BUSTLING BOROUGHS

Most people think of Manhattan when they think of New York City. But that's just one of the five boroughs that make up this bustling city. Here's more info on the other four boroughs.

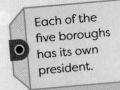
QUEENS

East of Manhattan and across the river is Queens, the largest borough by landmass. It is considered both the most ethnically diverse county in the US and the most culturally diverse urban area in the world.

BROOKLYN

Brooklyn is king. No, really—it's also known as Kings County. It is the biggest borough by population. Its historically Black neighborhoods, including Weeksville, Crown Heights, and Bed-Stuy, are an important part of New York's story.

STATEN ISLAND

The southernmost borough of New York City is an island unto itself. Staten Island is a quilt of lush parks, suburban neighborhoods, historic districts with Victorian houses, and one very large boardwalk.

STEP UP!

The Bronx has the most "step streets" in New York City, with over 60! These outdoor stairways allow walkers to navigate some of the borough's many hills. The longest, at West 230th Street, spans 295 feet (90 m) and climbs 38 feet (11.6 m) tall, combining three sets of steps and connecting four avenues.

THE BRONX

The Bronx is the northernmost borough and the only one connected to the US mainland. It is very residential, with thriving Black and Latinx communities. The Bronx is home to gems like Yankee Stadium, the Bronx Zoo, and Pelham Bay Park, the largest park in the whole city.

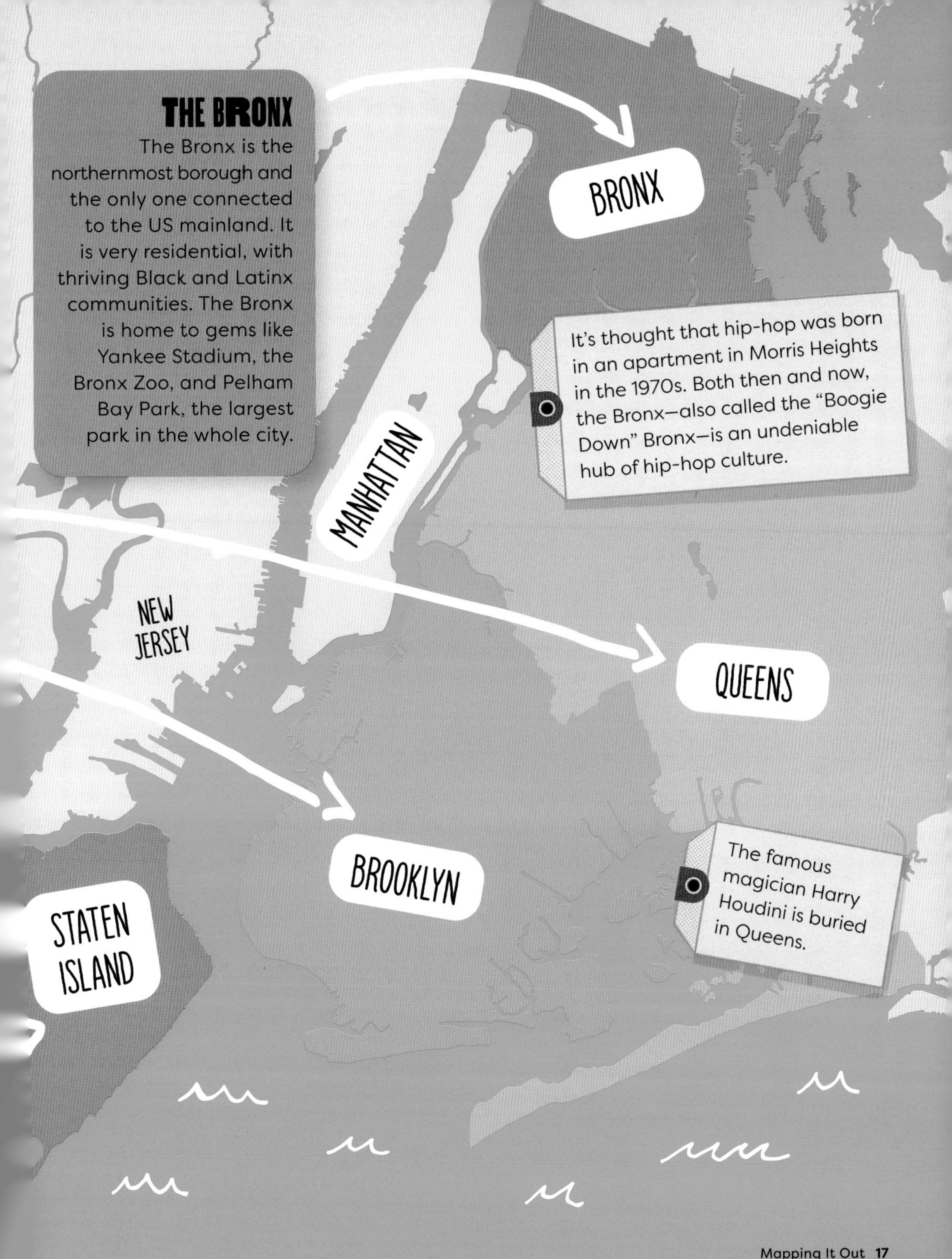

BRONX

MANHATTAN

It's thought that hip-hop was born in an apartment in Morris Heights in the 1970s. Both then and now, the Bronx—also called the "Boogie Down" Bronx—is an undeniable hub of hip-hop culture.

NEW JERSEY

QUEENS

BROOKLYN

STATEN ISLAND

The famous magician Harry Houdini is buried in Queens.

MEET THE SUBWAY

With 25 routes and more than 470 stations, the New York City subway is one of the best ways to get around the city. It's also the largest subway system in the United States. Hundreds of miles of tracks take riders far and wide!

Fast Facts

Amount of track: **665 miles (1,070 km)**

Daily riders: **over 3 million**

Busiest station: **Times Square**

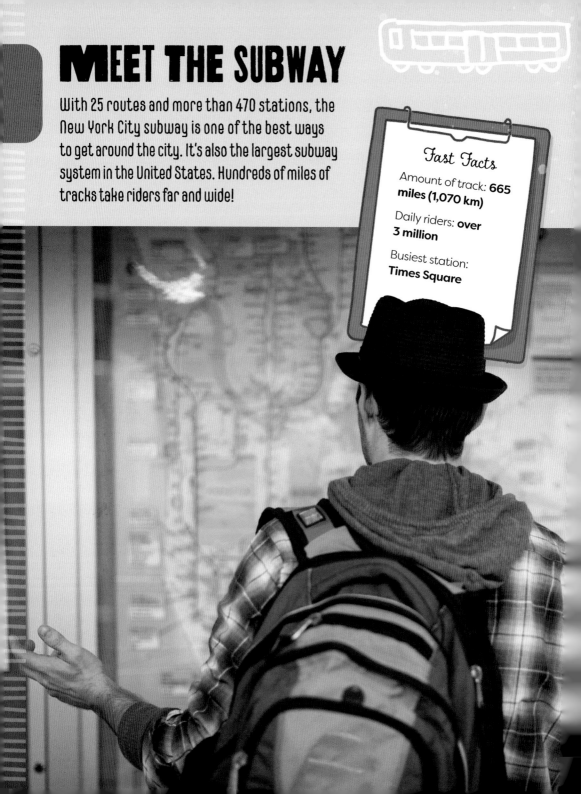

Downtown & Brooklyn ↴

Subway Map

Neighborhood Map

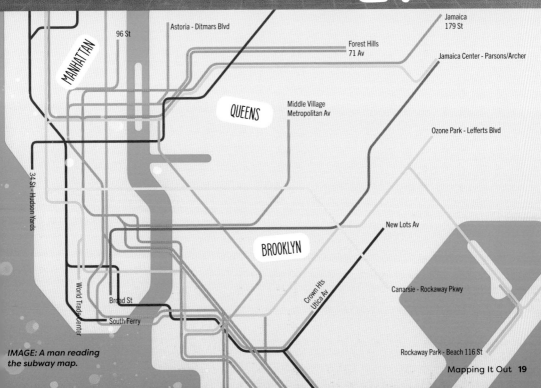

MANHATTAN

96 St

Astoria - Ditmars Blvd

Jamaica
179 St

Forest Hills
71 Av

Jamaica Center - Parsons/Archer

QUEENS

Middle Village
Metropolitan Av

Ozone Park - Lefferts Blvd

34 St - Hudson Yards

New Lots Av

BROOKLYN

World Trade Center

Broad St

South Ferry

Crown Hts
Utica Av

Canarsie - Rockaway Pkwy

*IMAGE: A man reading
the subway map.*

Rockaway Park - Beach 116 St

GETTING AROUND TOWN

IMAGE: A fleet of yellow taxis in busy traffic.

ON THE WATER

RIDE THE ORANGE FERRY

There are many ways people in and around New York City get from place to place. One popular way is by boat. The Staten Island Ferry has been taking passengers across New York Harbor between Manhattan and Staten Island for more than 200 years. Today, the boats are painted orange to stand out in heavy fog and snow. Hop on anytime (for free!) and check out amazing views of the Statue of Liberty and the city skyline. Like the city that never sleeps, neither does the ferry. It runs 24 hours a day, 365 days a year.

Fast Facts

Length of ferry route:
5.2 miles (8.4 km)

Ferry length:
310 feet (95 m)

Number of passengers per year: **15 million**

In the 1640s, Cornelius Dircksen became the first person to ferry people between Brooklyn and Manhattan—with his canoe!

THE STATEN ISLAND FERRY FLEET

There are five boats that make up the Staten Island Ferry's fleet. Together, these boats make almost 600 trips from Monday to Friday and carry 45,000 passengers. On weekends, the ferries make about 200 trips over two days. The 5.2-mile (8.4-km) route takes 30 minutes one way. In one year, the Staten Island fleet goes back and forth about 50,000 times. That's the same distance as going around the globe 17 times!

IMAGES: A bright yellow New York water taxi (left); the iconic Staten Island Ferry (above).

HIT THE ROAD

The city's longest bus ride, the S78 in Staten Island, runs for almost 20 miles (32 km).

RIDE THE BUS

There are more than 5,700 buses in NYC's "street fleet." In fact, it's the largest public transportation system in North America. Buses in this giant fleet travel on more than 200 local routes in the five boroughs. Bus fares are paid by a metro card, an app, or coins. No paper money is allowed. Why? Strong vacuum hoses are used to suck out everything in the fare boxes. Paper would get shredded to pieces by the suction! New York City's buses are a fun way to get around—you can see the city's many sights as you make your way to wherever you're going.

IMAGES: A NYC bus in Times Square (above); a yellow cab driving past Broadway theaters (opposite top); the city's bikeshare program allows riders to rent bikes stored at "docks" throughout the city (opposite bottom).

HAIL A CAB

NYC's taxis are immediately recognizable by their yellow color. They are the only vehicles that are allowed to pick up people hailing, or flagging down, a ride. In total, the cabs travel 70,000 miles (112,700 km) a year around city streets. That's the same as almost three times around the world.

For easy identification, all NYC taxis must be painted the now iconic yellow. It's the law!

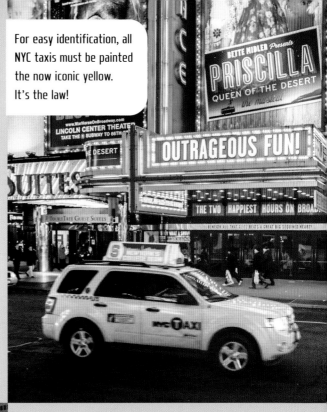

Fast Facts

Number of taxis:
more than 13,000

Average daily
taxi trips: **90,000
to 100,000**

New Yorkers who
regularly ride bikes:
more than 900,000

PEDAL POWER

Riding a bike, or cycling, is a popular and very green way to travel in this urban jungle, which provides 1,500 miles (2,414 km) of bike lanes. But for younger riders, there are greener spaces that make biking safe and more fun. Pelham Bay Park is the city's largest—three Central Parks could fit inside it. With 5 miles (8 km) of biking paths starting in the Bronx, it's a great place to use your pedal power!

TAKE THE TRAIN

What keeps the Big Apple running? It's definitely the New York City subway. Many of the first subway trains in NYC were above ground. Today, about 60 percent of the subway runs through underground tunnels on electric tracks.

There's always hustle and bustle in the stations—more than three million people ride the NYC subway each day, and each station is a world of its own. The music of buskers, or street performers, echoes along the platforms. Hundreds of mosaics capture the city's culture and history. There are even abandoned stations hidden in tunnels between stops. Some certainly have stories to tell, like **Track 61** under the Waldorf Astoria hotel that has a secret entrance, or the ornate **Old City Hall** station, decorated with glass tiles and chandeliers. It can be toured a few times a year if you can snag a ticket.

Train stations aren't the only things you'll find below New York's busy streets. What was once Court Street Station in downtown Brooklyn is now the hidden **Transit Museum**. You can take a ride through more than 100 years of history—and peek inside vintage train cars!

UNDER PRESSURE
Before the modern subway, NYC's first underground transit system—the Beach Pneumatic Transit—used air pressure to move cars. Strong bursts of air powered by a giant fan would "push" the train cars.

If the 665 miles (1,070 km) of train tracks in NYC were laid out end-to-end, they would reach all the way to Chicago.

STEP ON IT!

WALK THE GRID

Hey, we're walkin' here! Skip public transit and explore like a true New Yorker—on your feet. The street grid is Manhattan's defining characteristic. In 1811, city planners organized the city into rows of numbered avenues and streets. The tangled lanes of pre-grid districts—like the **West Village** or **Financial District**—are also fun to get lost in. Create your own tour with a neighborhood stroll or get a pigeon's point of view by walking across the major bridges and taking in the views. No matter where you go, there's no shortage of sidewalks in the city. NYC has more than 12,000 miles (19,300 km) of sidewalks—that's almost the distance from NYC to Perth, Australia!

IMAGES: Pedestrians exploring the Lower East Side neighborhood (above); the High Line on a sunny day (opposite top); a sign marking the Manhattan Waterfront Greenway (opposite bottom).

TAKE THE HIGH LINE

Some of the Big Apple's best spots can only be experienced on foot. One such place is **The High Line**, a 1.45-mile-long (2.3 km) public park that was once an elevated rail line. More than 500 species of plants and trees can be found here! Scenic overlooks, awesome art, tiny concerts, and tasty eats collide on this green bridge where miniature woodlands and green thickets sprout from steel tracks. Here, nature rules!

HIT THE GREENWAY

Get off the grid and onto the **Manhattan Waterfront Greenway**—a 32-mile (51-km) waterfront corridor divided into three sections along the East, Harlem, and Hudson Rivers. The longest, the Hudson River Greenway, includes walkways, bike paths, and plenty of places to take a break after a day of play. Nearly 7,000 bike riders use it every day. It's the busiest bikeway in the country! Manhattan's only lighthouse, the Little Red Lighthouse at Fort Washington Park, holds a festival each year with children's book readings and live music to celebrate the historic red building.

UNUSUAL RIDES

TRAM TO THE TOP

Take an aerial adventure on the **Roosevelt Island Tramway**, which connects Roosevelt Island in the East River to Manhattan's Upper East Side. Via cables, the tram zips roughly 3,000 feet (914 m) across the river at up to 17 miles per hour (27 km/h), giving passengers thrills and sky-high sights through huge windows. How high does it go? The tram reaches 250 feet (76 m) in the air! It was meant to be a temporary way for people to cross the river when it first opened in 1976, but the tram became so popular, it stayed. On the ride, the United Nations building can be seen way in the distance. Though it's in NYC, the UN is international territory!

IMAGES: A Roosevelt Island tram car over the East River (above); a pedicab navigating traffic (opposite top); the Central Park Boathouse and its reflection in the Lake (opposite bottom).

YOUR CARRIAGE AWAITS

A pedicab is a small carriage drawn by a person on a bike rather than a horse! These funky, human-powered three-wheeled vehicles can be found zipping around tourist hotspots like Times Square and Central Park. Many are customized with string lights and colorful decorations. Pedicabs are better for tours or entertainment than practical transport. There are about 850 in operation around the city.

When boat rides were first offered at the Central Park Boathouse, it cost only 40 cents for one hour!

ROW YOUR OWN WAY

Row, row, row your boat, gently down the ... city? If you want to enjoy some waterfront scenery, head to the **Central Park Boathouse** at the Lake, another of the city's public parks. Before it became the Lake, this area was a large swamp. Today, it's a bird-watcher's paradise. As you row around, look for swans, ducks, and even heron and egrets. If you're hungry after all the wildlife watching, head back to the Boathouse and grab a snack or treat!

PLACES TO PLAY

IMAGE: A sky-high view of Coney Island.

PLENTIFUL PLAYGROUNDS

SWELL SEWARD

Did you know that **Seward Park** in the Lower East Side was one of the country's first playgrounds? On opening day in 1903, more than 2,000 children raced there to play the day away, and the park still stands! Today, you can climb jungle gyms, splash in the water fountain, and swing to your heart's content. You'll also find a statue of Togo, a hero husky who, along with his team, saved lives by delivering medicine to people in remote Alaska when no one else could—a huge blizzard made travel too dangerous!

Seward Park was named after New Yorker William Seward, President Abraham Lincoln's secretary of state. He arranged for the purchase of Alaska to the US.

SWEET SITE

Domino Park Playground is one of a kind! Found on the Brooklyn waterfront, this colorful play place was inspired by the Domino Sugar Refinery, which once towered over the neighborhood. Actually, it's a miniature version of the old factory. There are silo towers and slides and plenty of spaces to play hide-and-seek. The top of the silos are the perfect place to look out over the water to spot boats and see the New York City skyline.

EXPLORE EGYPT

Okay, not really. You don't need to take a plane to feel like you've stepped out of the city and into Egypt's epic past. The architect who designed **Ancient Playground** in Central Park was inspired by the Metropolitan Museum of Art's Egyptian collection. Here, you can play on pyramids, a sundial, and an obelisk. But if you don't want to time travel, you can just hop on the swings!

AHOY, MATEY!

The competition is fierce, but the **Seaside Wildlife Nature Park** playground might be the city's biggest treasure. Surrounded by 20 acres (8 ha) of wilderness, this Staten Island playground transports visitors out of the marsh and into the sea. At this nautical-themed play zone, explore a mini lighthouse, climb atop an open-mouthed shark, or crawl inside a wooden shipwreck. Pirates and sailors welcome!

IMAGES: Children on the slides at Ancient Playground (above); kids dressed as pirates (right); Seward Park in the Lower East Side (opposite top); the factory-inspired Domino Park Playground (opposite bottom).

HANDS-ON MUSEUMS

LET'S GO!

BE THE BOSS

The **Brooklyn Children's Museum** is more than 120 years old! It was the first museum in the world to be dedicated exclusively to kids. Forget the glass-covered paintings and "don't touch" signs. Here, you can touch and play your way through the exhibits. Run your own kid-size shop based on real Brooklyn storefronts at the *World Brooklyn* exhibit. Then head to *AirMaze*, a gigantic, interactive pressurized air system with 250 feet (76 m) of tubes and blowers. Here, you can insert objects, such as scarves and balls, into the tubes and use valves to direct them as the air zips them around the tubes.

IMAGES: A child playing at the Brooklyn Children's Museum (above); on the deck of the USS Intrepid *(opposite top); a child making bubbles at a hands-on exhibit (opposite bottom).*

SKY'S THE LIMIT

Buckle your seat belts—the **Intrepid Museum** is built inside and around an actual aircraft carrier, the legendary *Intrepid*. This hulking craft on the Hudson River's Pier 86 houses a dizzying collection of historic aircraft, including fighter jets, a spy plane, and other astonishing airliners. Stop by the space shuttle *Enterprise* and explore inside the nuclear missile submarine *Growler* for history, science, and adventure. You can even hop in the pilot's seat of a helicopter and steer an airplane.

The fastest manned aircraft reached speeds of 4,520 miles per hour (7,274 km/h). At that speed, it could fly around the equator in 5.5 hours!

GET POPPING

Grab your goggles! The **New York Hall of Science (NYSCI)** in Queens is a hotspot for science and technology experiments. See, smell, touch, invent—there are hundreds of ways to play and learn. Check out *The Big Bubble Experiment*, where you can blow, stretch, and pop bubbles in all shapes and sizes. Hit the Science Playground where scientific principles meet principles of fun. NYSCI is always changing. But one thing's for sure: you'll never had this much fun while making new discoveries!

ESCAPE TO CONEY ISLAND

Fast Facts

Speed of the Cyclone roller coaster: **60 miles per hour (97 km/h)**

Length of track traveled in under two minutes: **2,640 feet (805 m)**

Biggest drop: **85 feet (26 m)**

Imagine a roller coaster with sea views! That's what you get at **Coney Island**, located on the southern tip of Brooklyn. It's home to NYC's largest amusement park, **Luna Park**, which is a maze of rides, games, and food on the Coney Island boardwalk. Next door is the 150-foot-tall (46 m) Wonder Wheel—a must ride—rising from **Deno's Wonder Wheel Amusement Park**.

This fun-filled island was also home to the world's first roller coaster. Inspired by coal-mining trains, the Gravity Switchback Railway opened in 1884. The Cyclone, a wooden roller coaster, opened in 1927 and still runs today. Back then, it cost only five cents to ride!

Thrill-seekers of all ages can enjoy what Coney Island has to offer—but you might want to wait on the hot dog until after the stomach-swooping fun.

IMAGE: The Cyclone towering over Luna Park.

THE MERMAID PARADE
To kick off every summer, thousands of aspiring mermaids and sea-themed revelers flood the shores of Coney Island for this annual parade. It is a *fin*-tastic mishmash of marching, dancing, quirky floats, handmade costumes, and marching bands. It's also a celebration of community, culture, art, and creativity.

HIT THE BEACH

Fast Facts

Total span of NYC public beaches:
14 miles (22 km)

Total coastline:
520 miles (837 km)

Number of city-maintained beaches in NYC: **8**

Seals visit the waters off NYC's beaches for easier fishing in winter. The waters farther north can be too icy!

THE BRIGHT SIDE

Brighton Beach is a section of shore and boardwalk just east of Coney Island and the perfect spot for a relaxing day at the beach. It's easy to get to and a great place to enjoy surf and sun—with suncreen, of course! The surrounding Brighton neighborhood is called "Little Odessa" after the Ukrainian city because it is the largest Russian- and Ukrainian-speaking community outside of eastern Europe. The borscht and meat *vareniki* (dumplings) are among the most authentic Russian food in NYC. Grab a beach umbrella—and a bite!

IMAGES: A calm day at Brighton Beach (above); two surfers walking the dunes of Rockaway Beach (opposite top); beachgoers with umbrellas relaxing at Jacob Riis Park (opposite bottom).

SURF'S UP!

Hang ten! **Rockaway Beach** is the city's only legal surfing spot. Surfers plunge into the sometimes-rough waters all year round. While walking around, watch your step! In May and June, hordes of horseshoe crabs use the beach as a breeding ground. Shorebirds are also close by, pecking at the ground looking for a meal. Nearby, Sandpiper Playground is named for the sandpiper birds that rest there during their migration. Some travel over 1,000 miles (1,609 km) before stopping at the beach!

BY THE BOARDWALK

Jacob Riis Park, located on the Rockaway Peninsula, opened in 1912—more than 110 years ago! Today, during summer, vendors sell delicious burgers, fries, and sweet treats along the one-mile (1.6-km) strip of boardwalk. It's the perfect place for ice cream after a day of watching the waves and taking a dip. While you relax, look up to see planes fly overhead as they land at nearby JFK Airport. Also nearby, at Floyd Bennett Field, the National Parks Service offers camping for kids!

SUPERB SPORTS

BATTER UP!

A visit to **Yankee Stadium** in the Bronx is a home run. On game nights, the arena becomes electric with the crack of bats, cheers from fans, and the zingy smell of fried foods in the air. Though the stadium is not the original structure, it's impossible not to imagine the most famous Yankees of all time out on the field—like Lou Gehrig, Mickey Mantle, and the iconic Babe Ruth. In honor of Babe Ruth, Yankee Stadium is nicknamed "The House That Babe Built." For a special treat, visit the somewhat secret memorabilia museum on-site. It opens 90 minutes before the first pitch.

Fast Facts

Yankee Stadium seating capacity: **about 46,000**

Home runs hit by Babe Ruth: **714**

Babe Ruth's jersey number: **3**

NYC TEAMS

New York is home to 11 professional sports teams, more than any other city in the US. Visitors can catch football, basketball, soccer, and even hockey games in the Big Apple.

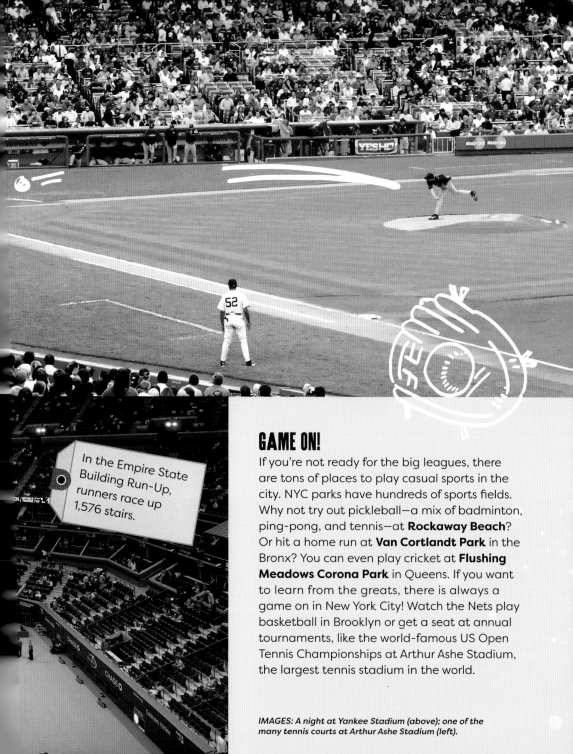

In the Empire State Building Run-Up, runners race up 1,576 stairs.

GAME ON!

If you're not ready for the big leagues, there are tons of places to play casual sports in the city. NYC parks have hundreds of sports fields. Why not try out pickleball—a mix of badminton, ping-pong, and tennis—at **Rockaway Beach**? Or hit a home run at **Van Cortlandt Park** in the Bronx? You can even play cricket at **Flushing Meadows Corona Park** in Queens. If you want to learn from the greats, there is always a game on in New York City! Watch the Nets play basketball in Brooklyn or get a seat at annual tournaments, like the world-famous US Open Tennis Championships at Arthur Ashe Stadium, the largest tennis stadium in the world.

IMAGES: A night at Yankee Stadium (above); one of the many tennis courts at Arthur Ashe Stadium (left).

GET CARRIED AWAY

CLASSIC CAROUSEL

NYC has loved carousels for more than a century. Brooklyn once had several carousel workshops where expert carvers brought the wooden horses and chariots on **Jane's Carousel** to life. The carousel itself was purchased from a company in Ohio and shipped to the city. It's now in Brooklyn Bridge Park, where the 48 colorful horses are ready to take riders for a spin.

INCREDIBLE INSECTS

Bug out at the Bronx Zoo! If your legs need a break from walking the town, the **Bug Carousel** is the perfect place to rest. Grab a seat atop a giant praying mantis, a grasshopper, or dung beetle, if you dare. There are plenty to choose from with 64 different hand-carved insects! While you're spinning, chill out to the carousel's soundtrack composed from real-life insect sounds and check out the painted murals depicting the stages of metamorphosis.

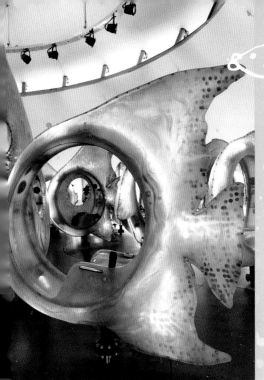

UNDER THE SEA

Battery Park in Manhattan is where you can find this seaworthy merry-go-round. While the **Seaglass Carousel** doesn't actually go under the water, its brightly colored fiberglass fish are lit up to give riders the feeling that they are swimming with glowing sea creatures in the shimmering waves. The pavilion is inspired by a nautilus shell. The sea theme honors the fact that the city's original aquarium once stood near this spot.

The first carousel in Central Park was powered by a horse or mule hidden in a compartment below the machine.

AN EPIC RIDE

The **Central Park Carousel**, found abandoned at Coney Island, was installed in the park's Children's District in 1951. With 57 hand-carved horses and two chariots, it hosts approximately 250,000 riders every year! As long as the weather allows, it spins seven days a week.

IMAGES: The Seaglass Carousel's shiny fish (above); a close-up of a colorful Central Park Carousel horse (right); a traditionally carved carousel horse (opposite top); the bug seats at the Bug Carousel (opposite bottom).

WHAT A VIEW!

IMAGE: The Charles Engelhard Court
in the Metropolitan Museum of Art.

SOAK IN THE SKYLINE

In the second-floor museum, you can take a picture with a replica of King Kong's hands ripping through the building.

THE EPIC EMPIRE

See for yourself why the **Empire State Building** is one of the most famous skyscrapers in the world. The 86th floor observatory deck curves around the iconic spire. Up here, visitors get a full-circle, open-air view of the Big Apple. If you're lucky enough to ascend when the sky is clear, you might be able to spy New Jersey or Connecticut through a classic viewfinder. A fancy glass elevator will bring you 16 floors higher to the Top Deck observatory on the 102nd floor!

IMAGES: The Empire State Building at night (above); sightseers taking in the view from Top of the Rock (opposite top); the view from One World Observatory (opposite bottom).

A ROCKIN' SIGHT

You don't need to be a mountain climber to get to the Top of the Rock—the observation terraces at the tip of **Rockefeller Center**, a building with its own zip code! Go up 70 floors for a bird's-eye view of the city below, as well as stunning skyline sights. You might even meet Roxy the Owl, the building's official mascot. Roxy was inspired by a real-life owl who chose to make a temporary home in Rockefeller Center's famous Christmas tree on the plaza!

Fast Facts

Time to the top of One World Trade Center by elevator: **47 seconds**

How far out you can see: **45 miles (72 km)**

Number of visitors: **10 million and counting**

OBSERVE AND REFLECT

On the 100th floor of **One World Trade Center** is One World Observatory, the highest point in New York City. This marvel of glass and mind-blowing geometry is the tallest building in the Western Hemisphere. It's 1,776 feet (541 m) tall in honor of the year the Declaration of Independence was signed. The structure was built on the site of the Twin Towers, which collapsed on September 11, 2001. The crowning spire has a specially crafted beacon of light that shines in memory of the victims of 9/11.

DOORWAY TO THE WORLD

PEER INTO THE PAST

Teenager Annie Moore from Ireland was the first immigrant to go through **Ellis Island** after it opened on New Year's Day in 1892. The last was Norwegian merchant Arne Petterson in 1954. Twelve million people arrived here over a span of 62 years. Many helped create the city of New York. You can visit the Wall of Honor, an interactive exhibit that stands where crowds of hopeful future Americans once gathered, and the National Museum of Immigration. Were your ancestors here? Visit the Family History Center, to find out!

Fast Facts

Height: **305 feet (93 m)**

Steps to the crown: **162 from the top of the pedestal**

Position: **southeast, in direct sight of ships entering the harbor**

VISIT LADY LIBERTY

Lady Liberty was a gift from France to mark the 100-year anniversary of US independence. But did you know the French also wanted to celebrate the recent abolition of slavery, which is why her foot has a broken shackle? It took 21 years to complete the **Statue of Liberty**, and getting her to the US was no easy task. She had to be taken apart, shipped, and reassembled. On Liberty Island, get up close and personal with this larger-than-life lady who was built to slightly sway in any direction in the wind. Here, you can check out the **Statue of Liberty Museum** and, with early reservations, even walk up to Lady Liberty's crown!

IMAGES: The entrance to the National Museum of Immigration (above); the Statue of Liberty holds her torch aloft in the New York Harbor (left).

MUSEUM MILE

AWE-WORTHY ART

New York City's famous Museum Mile is a stretch of Fifth Avenue that is home to the mega **Metropolitan Museum of Art**, also called the Met. Famous paintings, like Vincent van Gogh's *Self-Portrait with a Straw Hat*, are mandatory stops here. But at the Met, art isn't just a collection of paintings. The sprawling building holds a large number of pieces, including Grecian statues, ancient pottery, medieval armor, and the huge Temple of Dendur—a whole Egyptian temple! The smallest object is a seal (a type of stamp) from ancient Mesopotamia. It's a teeny-tiny 1.12-inch (2.8-cm) object and was likley used as a type of signature.

Fast Facts

Size of museum: **over 2,000,000 square feet (185,000 sq m)**

Size of blue whale model: **94 feet (29 m), 21,000 pounds (9,525 kg)**

Number of halls: **45**

WELL, NATURALLY!

The **American Museum of Natural History** makes solar system–size concepts entertaining and interactive. Visit the Hayden Planetarium to learn how planets form. Walk the 400-foot-long (122 m) Scales of the Universe to bounce between subatomic particles and galaxies. Flutter into the Butterfly Vivarium to see the life cycle of butterflies and moths. And venture to the dinosaur halls to witness the evolution of extinct beasts. Hi, *T. rex*! This playground of learning evolves with every new discovery made by its thousands of scientists

The museum's blue whale model gets a yearly bath. It takes three days to clean.

IMAGES: Visitors admiring Vincent van Gogh's paintings at the Met (above); the blue whale model inside AMNH's Hall of Ocean Life (left).

MARVELS IN MIDTOWN

A GRAND SIGHT

All aboard! New York City's premier train station is worth a stop, even if you don't have a ticket. Rising proudly from 42nd Street, **Grand Central Terminal** is a hive of history, architecture, food, fancy passages, and shops. But the most magnificent sight is above your head—the hand-painted Main Concourse Ceiling, a tapestry of gold-leaf constellations against vibrant blue skies and 2,500 stars. Some stars are even equipped with electric bulbs! The mural was painted backward as if its viewer is a celestial being looking down from the heavens rather than up.

Grand Central has 48 acres (19 ha) of basements. That's about 37 football fields! One, M42, is 13 stories deep.

Fast Facts

Building size: **390 feet (119 m) by 270 feet (82 m)**

Building space: **4 floors**

Single busiest day: **December 30, 1929, with 8,939 requested books**

BOOK IT!

There are 92 libraries in the **New York Public Library** system. The main branch on Fifth Avenue is a must-see. This unique building feels like a palace. It's even guarded by two grand lion statues. The library holds more than 54 million items—and not just books. Some treasures on display include the oldest copy of *The Tales of Mother Goose*, old and creepy Halloween cards from the early 20th century, and Christopher Milne's stuffed bear, the real Winnie the Pooh! For people with special requests, a conveyor belt—the "book train"—delivers reading materials to the library from an underground storage site in nearby Bryant Park.

The New York Public Library holds a draft of the Declaration of Independence, written in Thomas Jefferson's own handwriting.

IMAGES: Commuters hustling to their trains in Grand Central Terminal (above); the Rose Main Reading Room at the main branch of the NYPL (left).

BROOKLYN BRIDGE

Visible from the park's shore, Bird Island has a platform for ospreys looking to rest their wings. The island was made from an old railroad float transfer bridge, a structure once used to transport train cars across the harbor.

When people talk about the New York City skyline, they are often referring to Manhattan (right)—but Brooklyn's skyline is also amazing. A walk across the **Brooklyn Bridge** will give you majestic views of the borough's landmarks from afar. Can you see the green expanse of **Brooklyn Bridge Park**? Or the new Brooklyn Tower, whose dark facade pierces the sky like a villain's lair?

Of course, the bridge is a sight unto itself: its gothic arches, granite towers, and dizzying web of suspension cables are best viewed while you're on it, 100 feet (30 m) above the swirling East River. Be very still and see if you can feel the suspended bridge sway slightly with the natural flow of wind, water, and traffic below. Don't worry—it's supposed to do that. Your legs will be sore in the morning from all the walking, but the experience is worth it!

IMAGE: The brightly lit Brooklyn Bridge and glowing Manhattan skyline.

A MODEL BRIDGE

Before the Brooklyn Bridge was built, engineer John Roebling designed a smaller prototype. Roebling Bridge, connecting Ohio and Kentucky across the Ohio River, opened in 1867. When the Brooklyn Bridge—which is 6,016 feet (1,834 m)—opened in 1883, it was the longest suspension bridge in the world. Right away, people—and horse-drawn carriages—began using it. For the horses, it was easier than getting on a ferry!

LET'S EAT!

IMAGE: Towers of sesame, poppy seed, and cinnamon raisin bagels.

BORN IN NEW YORK

According to some, a cook invented the Chopped Cheese when he ran out of properly sized buns.

CHEESE, PLEASE!

New Yorkers are passionate about many things, especially their sandwiches. One such sandwich is the Chopped Cheese. This delicious meal consists of a ground beef patty, onions, adobo, and, yes, cheese! Ingredients are chopped together on the deli griddle and melted until the cheese is perfectly gooey. Transfer onto a classic roll, add lettuce, tomato, and condiments, and *voilà!* The C.C. was a neighborhood secret until word got out, and then people all over the city began to demand it. **Hajji's** (aka Blue Sky), a Harlem bodega, is almost certainly where it was created.

IMAGES: A freshly made Chopped Cheese (above); a chocolate egg cream (opposite top); General Tso's chicken over rice (opposite bottom).

DOWN THE HATCH

At first an egg cream might not sound like a tasty treat—until you hear what's really in it. The cold beverage has milk, chocolate syrup, and seltzer, mixed together for the *egg*-cellent signature froth. Like many New York City delicacies, there is no single story about how the dish was created. We do know it originated in the Lower East Side among Jewish immigrants more than 100 years ago. But how did the recipe with no egg or cream get its name? It's a mystery! **Russ & Daughters** on the Lower East Side is the place to go for this legendary drink.

Egg cream enthusiasts say authentic egg creams must be made with Fox's U-bet brand syrup. The company was founded in Brooklyn in 1900.

SWEET & SAVORY

Do you know about General Tso's chicken? This battered, saucy sweet-sour chicken rose to fame in NYC! A few decades ago, chef Peng Chang-kuei used typical flavors from Hunan, China, to invent General Tso's chicken. He later served the specialty in his Midtown Manhattan restaurant. But another chef, Tsung Ting Wang, might have put the chicken dish on his NYC menu first. Sometime during this food feud, sugar was added to the spicy, salty mix. This delicious twist made the chicken's popularity explode among sweet-toothed American diners.

NEW YORK STYLE

Fast Facts

Average cost of a slice: **$3.25**

Average cost of a one-topping pie: **$33.76**

GIMME A SLICE!

New York runs on pizza. Cheese glistening with grease. Perfect circles of pepperoni. New York–style pizza evolved from Neapolitan-style pizza, brought to the city by Italian immigrants in the 1900s. Authentic NY-style pizza is tossed by hand to achieve a thin crust, then topped with tomato sauce and fresh mozzarella. From the dollar slice to gourmet squid ink pizza, you can get all kinds of pie here. For a bite of history, **Lombardi's** in Little Italy has been making their pies since 1905—when a slice was just five cents. It's founder is credited with creating the style. Remember: if it's not foldable, it's not New York pizza!

IMAGES: Diners enjoying NY-style pizza (above); a bagel with lox, cream cheese, red onion, and capers (opposite top); hot dogs loaded with toppings (opposite bottom).

UNBEATABLE BAGELS

Hand-rolled New York bagels are a cut above the rest. Boiling gives the dough its signature dense, chewy texture. Poppy and sesame seed, pumpernickel, rye, even rainbow bagels—you can get everything here, including an *everything* bagel. Order like a New Yorker and grab one with lox (smoked salmon) and cream cheese schmear. This combo rose to popularity with Jewish immigrants along with the bagel itself. Iconic Jewish deli and grocery store **Zabar's** even boasts a locally famous lox-slicer, known for his incredibly-thin slices.

NYC tap water comes from the Catskill Mountains. It has a unique blend of minerals. Locals will tell you that's what makes their boiled bagels the best.

Apollo 7 astronauts enjoyed hot dogs on their way to the moon!

BUNS ON THE RUN

The meteoric rise of the hot dog started in 1867, when German immigrant and baker Charles Feltman wanted to give beachgoers a simple, savory food that didn't need silverware—and thus the "Coney Island Red Hot" was born. This twist on German "dachshund" sausage was later shortened to "hot dog." His bun business grew into an empire. At its peak of operation, Feltman's Ocean Pavilion sold up to 40,000 hot dogs daily! Today, these dogs can be found in grocery stores across the US. Like New York's best foods, hot dogs can be eaten on the go!

ON THE GO

MEALS WITH WHEELS

The city has a reputation for being, well, smelly. Some of those scents are the delicious aromas wafting up from the cooktops of food carts. Selling everything from shellfish to pickles to pretzels, food carts uphold a long tradition of mobile meals with immigrant roots. A popular staple is halal food (meals prepared according to Islamic practices), which usually involves a combo of rice and meat slathered with sauce. No winter stroll is complete without the irresistible sugary smell of roasted cashews, almonds, and peanuts from a Nuts 4 Nuts cart. Food carts are a diverse, dynamic, and delectable representation of the ever-changing city.

QUICK BITES

At New York delis, sandwiches piled high with sliced meats are top dog—but one item is a true hero: the BEC! These three magic letters stand for bacon, egg, and cheese. This fan favorite can also be found at an NYC bodega, a corner store that sells snacks, drinks, and other convenience items. Bodegas are open late (or all night), making them essential to the city that never sleeps. Not all bodegas have deli counters or hot food, but you can always get a bag of chips for snacking emergencies!

Fast Facts

Average visitors to Queens Night Market: **up to 20,000**

Number of countries represented at the Night Market: **at least 90**

FEAST YOUR EYES

Not full yet? Browse to your stomach's content at an indoor or outdoor vendor market. **Essex Market**, the city's oldest, began in 1818 as a group of covered food stalls in the Lower East Side. Today, it still has arguably the best pickles in the city. For modern munchies, Brooklyn's **Smorgasburg** provides food fusion, like the famous ramen burger. Night owls can make the trip to Flushing for the **Queens International Night Market**. Your jerk chicken or ice jelly might come with a concert!

IMAGES: Close-up of a BEC sandwich (above); a smoky grill at Smorgasburg in Brooklyn (left); a street vendor waits for customers at his food cart (opposite).

TAKE A SEAT

STORIED SANDWICHES

The sandwiches at **Katz's Delicatessen** are huge! They're filled with specially made corned beef and pastrami, which are very slowly cured for ultimate flavor—it takes 30 days! After the deli opened in 1888, it quickly became a neighborhood hotspot, and that hasn't changed. Today, people continue to line up around the block of this no-frills food paradise for the corned beef, brisket, and pastrami on rye. If you're not in town, Katz's delivers all over the United States!

FAMOUS FRANKS

Remember Mr. Feltman, the hot dog entrepreneur (see page 63)? A Feltman bun slicer Nathan Handwerker started his own hot dog venture in 1916. His first hot dogs sold for five cents each. Today, **Nathan's Famous** franks are found all over the world. Plus, the original location is still open on Coney Island! Equally famous is the Nathan's annual Fourth of July International Hot Dog Eating Contest. Participants have 10 minutes to eat as many hot dogs—and buns—as they can while more than 40,000 people watch!

SOUL FOOD

Experience royalty in Harlem at **Sylvia's Restaurant**, founded by the "Queen of Soul Food," Sylvia Woods, in 1962. What started as a small luncheonette made a name for itself with unmatched homestyle cooking—think barbecue ribs, mac 'n' cheese, collards—and it grew into a phenomenon. But despite its fame, Sylvia's still feels like home for the people of Harlem. It has been a community gathering place for decades.

TEA TIME

During its earliest days, the **Nom Wah Tea Parlor** was an oasis of tea, almond cookies, and mooncakes— which were made with special wooden molds so each little cake was perfectly shaped like the moon. Symbols on top were a clue to the filling inside! Today, the restaurant is also known for its dim sum. Nom Wah opened in 1920 on Doyers Street, which has a sharp elbow-shaped curve. No cars are allowed here, so everyone can walk freely!

IMAGES: Outside Sylvia's on Lenox Avenue in Harlem (above); diners wait for a table at Nom Wah (right); pastrami on rye at Katz's Deli (opposite top); the annual hot dog eating contest in Coney Island (opposite bottom).

SWEET TREATS

Fast Facts

Average width of a black and white:
4 inches (10 cm)

Cronut invented:
2013

Average length of first Cronut lines:
150 people

PASTRY PARADISE

Infinite confections line the streets of New York City. Stop in for a buttercream-frosted cupcake at **Magnolia Bakery**, or sample delicious cheesecake at **Junior's Restaurant**. At **Veniero's** Italian bakery, visitors can buy cannoli and *pastacroce* by the pound. Whoa! NYC's most famous sweet treat is called the black and white. It's part chocolate, part vanilla, both cookie and cake, and 100 percent yummy! If you're in the mood for something more adventurous, city bakers are always inventing new pastry crazes. Have a Cronut—a croissant and doughnut in one. The options are endless! What will you try first?

IMAGES: Freshly baked black and white cookies (above); the colorful displays at Economy Candy (opposite top); taiyaki filled with soft serve ice cream (opposite bottom).

SUGAR RUSH

Did you know Tootsie Rolls were invented in Brooklyn? Dots, Peeps, and other iconic candies were created here, too! Brooklyn once produced mind-boggling amounts of sugar at the Domino Sugar Refinery. All that sweetness brought lots of candy shops! **Economy Candy** has been around since the 1930s. This rainbow paradise sells 2,000 types of candy—from traditional jelly beans to vintage candy bars to the newest trending treats. You can even shop by color!

Häagen-Dazs ice cream was first sold in the Bronx—from horse-drawn wagons!

CUP OR CONE?

According to records, George Washington loved ice cream so much that one summer he spent hundreds of dollars on ice cream-making equipment. Today, you can find many ice cream parlors in New York City selling an array of inventive flavors. Feeling fancy? Check out the Golden Opulence Sundae at **Serendipity 3**—for an eye-popping $1,000! For a savory twist, sample flavors like almond cookie, *don tot* (egg custard), and pandan (a yummy tropical plant) at **Chinatown Ice Cream Factory**. Other Asian-inspired shops offer hand-rolled ice cream or scoops in a *taiyaki*—a fish-shaped waffle. What a catch!

HEADING TO BROADWAY

THE GREAT WHITE WAY

The first "modern" musical was performed in New York City in 1927. Soon after, the **Theater District** sprouted along the section of Broadway between 41st and 53rd Streets. It earned the nickname The Great White Way for its electric signs and brilliant lights. Today, we simply call it Broadway, but it hasn't lost its shine.

Modern Broadway shows feature elaborate sets and even fireworks that take the audience to another world. The term "Broadway" is more about size than location. A true Broadway theater has at least 500 seats. The largest has almost 2,000!

Ever wish you could go backstage? The **Museum of Broadway** has a one-of-a-kind collection of real costumes and set pieces from the most popular Broadway shows ever, like *Annie*, *The Lion King*, and *Hamilton*. Visitors learn the secrets of the Theater District, including the people and jobs that make the shows possible. Here, you have front-row seats to Broadway history. Curtains up!

Fast Facts

Longest-running show of all time: **The Phantom of the Opera (35 years!)**

Number of theaters actually located on Broadway: **3**

IMAGE: Times Square intersection (previous page); people exploring Manhattan's Theater District.

HIP, HIP, HIPPODROME!

Now demolished, the Hippodrome in NYC was once one of the world's largest theaters. The building's name was inspired by ancient Greek hippodromes, which were stadiums where spectators could watch chariot races. In the early 1900s, the theater hosted circus acts and ice ballets. It even had a water tank for high divers and aqua dancers!

Early theaters used large fans that blew air over giant blocks of ice to cool down the auditoriums.

BEYOND THE SHOWS

Fast Facts

Full length of Broadway: **33 miles (53 km)**

Length of Broadway in Manhattan: **13 miles (21 km)**

Original width: **80 feet (24 m) (Thus, "broad way"!)**

OFF THE GRID

Broadway is a thoroughfare that dates back to the 1600s—it was once the Wickquasgeck Trail, a path carved in the wilderness by Native Americans. Today, it runs the length of Manhattan, cutting through blocks with a diagonal slant. Traveling uptown (north) gives you a front-row seat to the Financial District, dazzling Times Square, Lincoln Center, and more. The street winds north toward Harlem, a beating heart of African American culture, then passes through Washington Heights (Little Dominican Republic) and into the Bronx. It keeps going for another 18 miles (29 km)!

YES, YOU MAY

You will find all kinds of shopping on Broadway. From north to south, you can browse souvenir stalls in Chinatown, cool clothing stores in SoHo, elaborate window displays in Midtown, and street vendors in Times Square. New York's most iconic department store, **Macy's**, is located on Broadway at Herald Square. It takes up almost the entire city block, making it the largest department store in the country!

WHO NEEDS A STAGE?

If Broadway is the spine of the city, plazas are its bones. Broadway connects several important squares—including Union Square, Madison Square, and Herald Square—and Columbus Circle. These open public spaces are hotspots for street performers, often called buskers. At any moment, you can catch concerts, acrobat shows, magicians, dancers, and plenty of surprising talent. One busker has even been known to haul a piano into Washington Square Park. You don't need a ticket for these shows. Just consider leaving a tip!

IMAGES: Character balloons at the iconic Macy's Thanksgiving Day Parade (above); Columbus Circle, located at the corner of Central Park (left); a view of Times Square (opposite).

AMAZING ARCHITECTURE

Fast Facts

Age: **more than 300 years**

Size of archives: **more than 2,000 feet (609 m) of historical records**

Church members: **some 1,600**

HISTORIC CHURCH

Trinity Church on Broadway is steeped in early American history. It's the place where George Washington attended services at St. Paul's Chapel after being sworn in as the nation's first president. The churchyard holds history, too. It's the resting place for many famous figures, including Alexander Hamilton, the first US secretary of the treasury. To bring the past vivdly to life, visitors can take an augmented reality (AR) tour!

WRINKLE FREE

The **Flatiron Building** is a marvel to behold. According to NYC legend, the shape of this striking triangular building was inspired by an actual clothes iron. That isn't exactly true—the odd shape of the plot influenced its construction. Lodged between Broadway and Fifth Avenue, its prow juts toward Madison Square Park. At its narrowest point at the very top, the building is just 6.5 feet (2 m) wide!

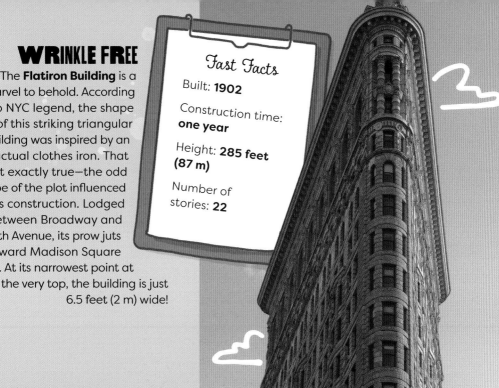

Fast Facts

Built: **1902**

Construction time: **one year**

Height: **285 feet (87 m)**

Number of stories: **22**

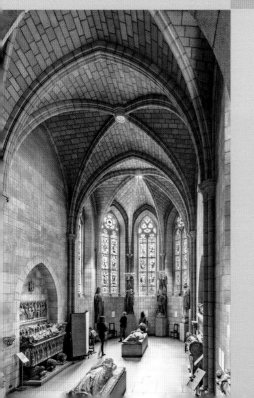

MEDIEVAL HAUNT

Follow Broadway all the way north until you find forested hills—and a medieval monastery! **The Cloisters**, the Metropolitan Museum of Art's second location, sits atop a tall hill in Fort Tyron Park at the very tip of Manhattan. Entering these quiet halls made of stone will give you chills. Here, medieval architecture and stained glass help transport visitors back in time to the Middle Ages. Hunt for the fabulous Unicorn Tapestries. The woven works of art depicting mythological horned horses are simply magic!

IMAGES: Looking up at the Flatiron Building (above); inside the Cloisters in Upper Manhattan (left); Trinity Church in Lower Manhattan (opposite).

TOUR TIMES SQUARE

Before electricity changed the world, Times Square bustled with horse-drawn stagecoaches! It was the introduction of public transportation that charted its very bright future. Knowing the newly invented subway would bring crowds to this central location, the owner of the *New York Times* decided to make the area—then known as Longacre Square—the home of the newspaper's headquarters. In 1904, it was officially renamed Times Square.

Today, millions flock here to stand at the center of the urban universe among theater stars, hustling merchants, street performers, and brilliant lights.

Almost hidden among it all are constantly changing artworks, such as murals and sculptures, that capture New York's creative side.

Times Square is not a square at all. It is a "bowtie"—named for the crisscross intersection of Broadway and Seventh Avenue.

IMAGE: The heart of Times Square.

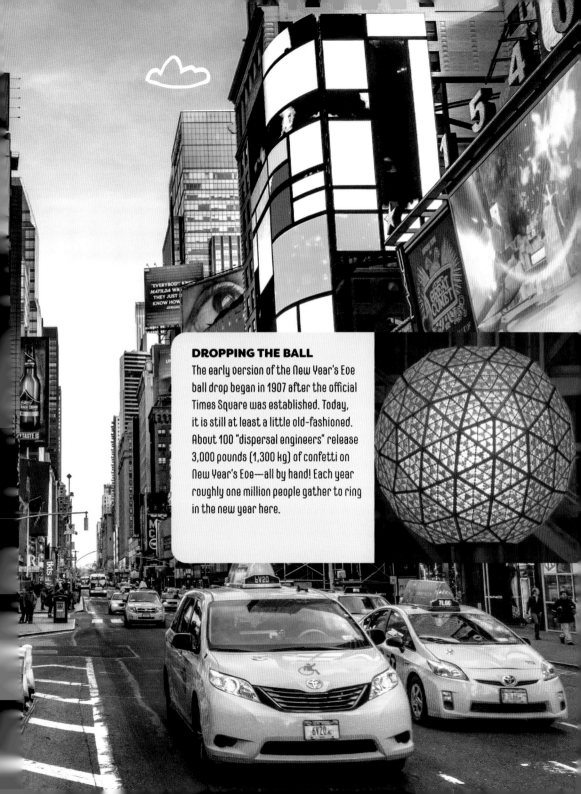

DROPPING THE BALL

The early version of the New Year's Eve ball drop began in 1907 after the official Times Square was established. Today, it is still at least a little old-fashioned. About 100 "dispersal engineers" release 3,000 pounds (1,300 kg) of confetti on New Year's Eve—all by hand! Each year roughly one million people gather to ring in the new year here.

OFFBEAT OFFERINGS

COMEDY CENTRAL

GO OFF SCRIPT

Sweeping stage shows exist outside of Broadway, too. With 100 to 499 seats, off-Broadway theaters are smaller than their big siblings—but their shows are just as spectacular. An off-Broadway ticket can mean anything from a bubble-blowing show to a mind-blowing magic show to beloved long-running spectacles like the Blue Man Group. Even *Sesame Street* has had an off-Broadway musical! This is where you can get a sneak peek at tomorrow's best shows, as many off-Broadway shows are training for the Broadway big leagues!

The intersection of Broadway and West 63rd Street is officially named Sesame Street.

THAT'S FUN!

PULL THE STRINGS

New York has a plethora of puppet shows to entertain kids of all ages. The **Swedish Cottage Marionette Theatre** in Central Park produces shows based on children's classic stories. **Teatro SEA** offers bilingual puppet performances that reflect the city's diverse puppetry traditions. **PuppetMobile** is a traveling group that puts on free shows and puppet-making workshops in parks. Then there's the awesome Jim Henson exhibit at the **Museum of the Moving Image** in Queens. Here, there are storyboards, scripts, and puppets from the Muppets' creator himself.

IMAGES: Members of the Blue Man Group at Beacon Theater, New York, NY (above); a puppet show (left).

KALEIDOSCOPE OF CULTURE

IMAGE: A scene from Spring Festival, also known as Chinese or Lunar New Year.

FOOD FUSION

The city's only remaining wooden pagoda roof stands on Mott Street, Chinatown's oldest street.

TASTY CHINATOWN

In Manhattan's **Chinatown**, centered on Canal and Mott Streets, narrow roads lined with restaurants, shops, neon signs, and bakeries serving meat and red bean-filled buns are booming. Markets display glistening fruits, dried goods, and silvery fish on ice, while street vendors gather in Forsyth Plaza to sell fruits and veggies of all kinds. An array of Shanghainese, Cantonese, Szechuan, Thai, and Asian fusion fare, as well as festivals and museums, keep the diverse cultures alive. Just as significant are the descendants of Asian immigrants who are making their own traditions.

Bronx's Little Italy still celebrates Ferragosto, an ancient Roman festival that has been celebrated for 2,000 years!

THANK YOU!

Fast Facts

Size: **about 2 square miles (5 sq km)**

Population: **about 150,000**

Established: **1870s**

ITALIAN EATS

North of Chinatown, on a short stretch of Mulberry Street, is **Little Italy**. At only five blocks, it's smaller than it once was—several decades ago, it covered around 50 blocks—but the neighborhood still packs a punch. During the annual Feast of San Gennaro, the streets explode with zeppole (Italian doughnut) and sausage vendors, cannoli-eating contests, live music, games and rides, and colorful floats. Food and fun all in one! For even more irresistible Italian flavors, head to the Bronx's Little Italy, where you can chow down on fresh pasta and bocconcini (mozzarella balls) at the historic neighborhood market.

IMAGES: A diner enjoys steamed dumplings in Chinatown (above); crowds flock to the Feast of San Gennaro in Little Italy (left).

NATIVE ROOTS

Did you know that Native Americans from the Mohawk tribe worked on several skyscrapers, including the Empire State Building? Or that Native American tribes were the first to live on Manhattan Island? The Lenape people called their island *Manahatta*. They and other groups fished, grew food, and were the first to navigate what was a wild landscape.

When Europeans colonized the area, it resulted in loss of life, lands, and traditions for Indigenous peoples. But their legacy cannot be denied—it is everywhere you look, especially in modern place-names. The Shorakapok Preserve uses the Native term for the fertile north end of the island, which means "sitting down place."

The **National Museum of the American Indian** helps preserve the history of Indigenous communities in New York City. Gallery displays tell their often overlooked stories, and the imagiNATIONS Activity Center allows kids to test Native inventions that are now woven into daily life. At the museum shop, you can take home jewelry, books, art, or clothing made by Native artisans.

IMAGE: An illustration of Native American longhouses on Manhattan Island from the 16th or early 17th centuries.

Wall Street is named for the wall that once stood there to bar Native Americans and the British from Dutch settlements.

WHAT'S IN A WORD?

Manhattan's Pearl Street gets its name from a Lenape midden—a giant mound of shucked oyster shells. The Lenape called today's Battery Park *Kapsee*, which translates to "sharp rock place." And *Shatemuc*, or "the river that flows both ways," was the Lenape term for the Hudson River. The tide causes the river to flow both north and south, depending on the time of day!

LOCAL LINGO

New York City English is its own official dialect—or variety—of English.

THE QUEENS WAY

Celebrate cultures in Queens! Here, many street and shop signs are written in non-English alphabets, and it's easy to hear multiple languages being spoken in the neighborhoods surrounding the **Queens Museum** and **Flushing Meadows Corona Park**. Places of worship are also a hub of native languages, like the **Hindu Temple Society of North America** in Flushing. Looking for a multicultural concert or festival? **Flushing Town Hall** is your place. There are so many countries represented by residents, that the **Queens Public Library** offers live phone interpreting in more than 240 languages!

More than 100 West African languages are spoken in the Bronx alone. At least 10 are endangered—perhaps more.

LANGUAGES AT RISK

Did you know that languages could go extinct? It's true—and New York City is the last refuge of some of these endangered languages. One Himalayan language, Seke, only has about 700 speakers in the world, and 150 of them live in or around two buildings in Brooklyn. The **Endangered Language Alliance** is helping to protect Seke and other languages that are in danger. Take a guided tour with them to find out more. To see an interactive visual of what's spoken where all over NYC, check out the Languages of New York City map!

IMAGES: *A South Asian shop in Jackson Heights, Queens (above); Korean dancers in Flushing, Queens (left).*

EXCITING EXHIBITS

EDIBLE ART?

At the **Museum of Food and Drink**, visitors can smell, touch, and—yes—taste their way through exhibits. Food scientists and culinary historians work to develop ever-changing displays that highlight foods that are cultural staples. Mouthwatering examples include a deep dive into the science of Indian curries and the history of Chinese-American restaurants. For the museum's grand opening, they brought out a massive puffing gun—the machine that creates (and puffs!) your favorite cereals—for samples. Here, even the pickiest of eaters will find something to munch on!

IMAGES: Stacks of paper take-out containers at MOFAD (above); a street view of the Three Kings Day celebration in East Harlem (opposite top); a German shorthaired pointer poses at the dog museum (opposite bottom).

SPANISH HARLEM'S HEART

Located at the northern end of Museum Mile is **El Museo del Barrio**. *El barrio*—"neighborhood" in Spanish—is East Harlem, or Spanish Harlem. This modern museum displays and preserves Latin-American and Caribbean art and culture. It is filled with art, but that's not all. It offers events in Spanish and English, and it's the perfect place to enjoy a fantastic festival. You can also take a virtual tour that highlights real-life locations, like the Graffiti Hall of Fame and local cuchifritos (fried foods) spots, for free!

The El Museo del Barrio hosts an annual Three Kings Day Parade each January 6. The celebration includes a parade led by three giant puppets.

TOP DOG

The towering Kalikow building on Park Avenue is home to one tail-wagging spot: the **The AKC Museum of the Dog**! Here, man's best friend is celebrated with fun and interactive exhibits showcasing the bond between humans and our furry companions. You can meet the breeds, learn about dogs with jobs, and even get matched with the perfect dog breed for you! An activity table allows visitors to create their own doggie art. Many are chosen to be displayed on the Community Wall—a display dedicated to dog lovers everywhere.

CELEBRATE YEAR-ROUND

MARK THE MONTH

Spring Festival, also called Lunar or Chinese New Year, is based on the ancient Chinese calendar and marked by the animals of the zodiac. Unlike other city festivities, it is celebrated for a whole month. During February, it's not uncommon to see traditional red envelopes and decorations all over the five boroughs. The Queens Botanical Garden hosts an annual lion dance performance. Chinatown's parade brings dragon dancing, elaborate costumes, festival booths, and even a talent show!

Fast Facts

Year of first parade:
1958

Average spectators:
1 million

Size of Puerto Rican community in NYC:
over 1 million people

PUERTO RICO ROCKS!

Every June, the **National Puerto Rican Day Parade** marches down Fifth Avenue in Manhattan in honor of Puerto Ricans and their rich heritage. Thought to be the biggest cultural parade in the country, this celebration features seas of waving flags, coasting colorful floats, and upbeat music around every corner. And don't miss the **152nd Street Cultural Festival** in the Bronx with music performances, dancing, face painting, and tons of fun.

IMAGES: Chinese dragons at the Spring Festival (above); marchers in the National Puerto Rican Day Parade (left); people celebrating Pride (opposite top); New York City Marathon runners (opposite bottom).

SHOW YOUR PRIDE

New York City gathers every June for this annual celebration of the queer community. In addition to uplifting LGBTQIA+ individuals of all cultures, ages, and races, the **Pride March** is a civil rights demonstration. The first march was held in 1970, in response to the Stonewall Uprising in Greenwich Village in 1969. Today, Pride is a vibrant, brave, and radical collection of marchers who assemble to honor the past and present of queer communities—and work toward a future without discrimination.

Fast Facts

Finishers in 1970: **55**

Finishers in 2023: **51,453**

Average race time: **4:39:47**

Fastest race time: **2:04:58**

RUN THE CITY

Fifty years ago, the **New York City Marathon** was a humble footrace held in Central Park. Today, that local competition is the world's largest marathon. It brings thousands of international athletes to New York City every year—not to mention the diverse crowds who line the city streets to cheer the competitors on. These courageous runners are united in one goal: to complete the 26.2-mile (42.2-km) course through all five boroughs. On your marks, get set—go!

THE WILD SIDE

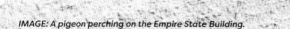
IMAGE: A pigeon perching on the Empire State Building.

FLY AWAY HOME

Fast Facts

Average length of pigeon: **12 to 14 inches (30 to 35 cm)**

Estimated NYC pigeon population: **more than 1 million**

Pigeon species throughout the world: **289**

THE GREAT FLYWAY

Prepare to be shocked—New York City is incredible for bird-watching! It's located in the perfect spot along the Atlantic Flyway, an ancient bird migration route. The city is an avian superhighway of songbirds, waterfowl, and shorebirds, and each season brings different species to watch. The **Wild Bird Fund** on the Upper West Side provides care for thousands of injured birds every year. Many are migrating individuals who need help or healing on their long journeys.

URBAN RAPTORS

NYC's bountiful birds include the fiercest of all—raptors! Peregrine falcons, ospreys, red-tailed hawks, and American kestrels thrive in the trees, tall buildings, and ponds perfect for picking off fish. Every borough has multiple hawk hotspots. In a heartwarming—and epic—story of survival, bald eagles have begun to nest within the city after nearly going extinct. Raptors are not only awesome, but they're a sign that New York's waterways are healthy—if there were no healthy fish, the birds wouldn't show up.

Peregrines nest in bridges, and red-tails relax on poles and window ledges.

PIGEONS ABOUND!

The story of the pigeon is a quintessential New York tale. The birds were first brought here from Europe (as a food source!) but quickly struck out on their own. They owned the town in no time at all—what is NYC today without their gray plumage or chorus of coos? Over the centuries, New Yorkers have raised pigeons on rooftops, shooed pigeons, fed pigeons, and even raced pigeons. NYC pigeons were also once birds with jobs! They were used during both world wars to transport messages between troops. Some received medals for their service!

IMAGES: A hawk at Yankee Stadium (above); pigeons pecking for food on an NYC sidewalk (left); terns taking a break by the riverside (opposite).

AMAZING ANIMALS

IT'S A JUNGLE!

The urban jungle meets the real jungle in the New York City zoos. Each borough has its own, with unique wildlife habitats, species, and animal activities. The **Queens Zoo** is home to the pudu, the world's tiniest—and possibly most adorable—deer species. The **Staten Island Zoo** has a horse barn and a bee apiary! After helping to train seals at the **Prospect Park Zoo**, pop next door and visit Brooklyn Botanic Garden—but watch out for the wandering peacocks. With opportunities to feed goats, sheep, and pigs, the Tisch Children's Zoo inside the **Central Park Zoo** is especially fun. Plus, it has the only cow in Manhattan!

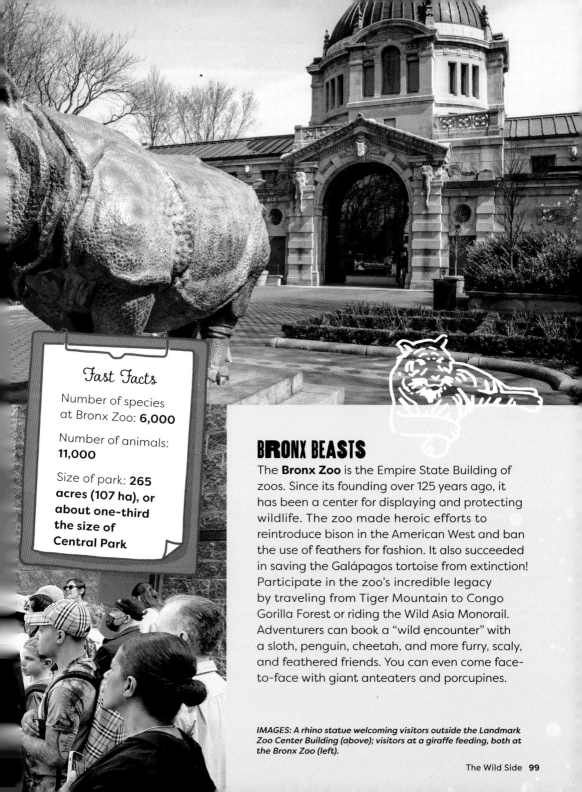

BRONX BEASTS

The **Bronx Zoo** is the Empire State Building of zoos. Since its founding over 125 years ago, it has been a center for displaying and protecting wildlife. The zoo made heroic efforts to reintroduce bison in the American West and ban the use of feathers for fashion. It also succeeded in saving the Galápagos tortoise from extinction! Participate in the zoo's incredible legacy by traveling from Tiger Mountain to Congo Gorilla Forest or riding the Wild Asia Monorail. Adventurers can book a "wild encounter" with a sloth, penguin, cheetah, and more furry, scaly, and feathered friends. You can even come face-to-face with giant anteaters and porcupines.

IMAGES: A rhino statue welcoming visitors outside the Landmark Zoo Center Building (above); visitors at a giraffe feeding, both at the Bronx Zoo (left).

AQUATIC WONDERS

The **New York Aquarium** in Coney Island actually shimmers—it's made from 33,000 aluminum tiles that dart and shine in the wind like a school of fish! The inside is swimming with sea otters, sharks, rays, octopuses, and other unbelievable sea creatures from moon jellies to zombie worms.

The Aquatheater puts on sea lion shows while the PlayQuarium lets visitors interact with marine habitats. One of the aquarium's many conservation projects is shark tagging and monitoring.

That's right—about 25 species of our toothy friends call New York waters home, including the shortfin mako and blue shark. The aquarium's team also spies on humpback whales to record whale songs to better understand how they live. And for the first time in years, wild dolphins have been spotted splashing in the Bronx River!

IMAGE: A visitor walks through the observation tunnel at the New York Aquarium.

REDBIRD REEFS

Since 2001, the Metropolitan Transportation Authority has plunged some 2,500 "retired" Redbird subway cars into the Atlantic Ocean. The goal? Create spaces for sea creatures to flourish. Now these artificial subway reefs are a rich habitat for sea life. No MetroCard required!

Healthy oceans need sharks.

CELEBRITY WILDLIFE

FLACO THE OWL

Behold: here's a bird's tale of intrigue and adventure. In 2023, a Eurasian eagle owl named Flaco escaped the Central Park Zoo. Being born and raised in captivity, it was thought that Flaco couldn't survive. But time after time, he evaded capture by the zookeepers who were desperately trying to bring him home. When the entire city realized Flaco was determined to make it in the Big Apple, the zoo officially stopped their mission to recapture him. After nine months in Central Park, Flaco began visiting rooftops and window ledges all over Upper Manhattan. When Flaco sadly passed away in 2024, New Yorkers made a memorial with flowers, photos, and handmade illustrations in his beloved park to honor his memory.

PALE MALE

Another city legend is Pale Male, the red-tailed hawk that made NYC his home for several decades. In 1991, Pale Male nested on the ledge of a luxury Fifth Avenue apartment building and never left the borough. New Yorkers were upset when construction workers "evicted" him for a construction project. Despite the perils of city living, Pale Male soldiered on, fathering an estimated 30 chicks and inspiring books, artwork, and at least one documentary. If you spot a red-tail in NYC, it's possible you could be seeing this feathered icon's lineage!

Fast Facts

Average elevation of a red-tailed hawk nest: **13 to 70 feet (4 to 21 m)**

Number of red-tailed hawk nests in Manhattan: **anywhere from 5 to 20 every year**

BODEGA CATS

Manager or *meowager*? While you're grabbing chips and water, you can make a feline friend at your local bodega. Bodega cats can be found purring, lounging, and licking their paws at corner stores all over the city. Originally introduced as a form of pest control, bodega cats range from mixed breed adopted cats to semi-feral cats that take up residence in the aisles and never leave. Technically, they are not allowed anywhere consumable food is sold. But if there's no grill, they are free to take up residence among stocked coolers and bags of rice!

IMAGES: *Pale Male on the balcony of a Fifth Avenue apartment building (above); a cat relaxing in front of an NYC store (left); Flaco the Eurasian eagle owl in Central Park (opposite).*

OUR "PEST" FRIENDS

Fast Facts

Estimated NYC rat population: **3 million**

Pizza Rat video views: **12 million and counting**

Average rat length: **12 to 16 inches (30 to 40 cm)— including the tail**

Amazing swimmers, rats can tread water for several days straight.

OH, RATS!

Another unofficial city mascot is the rat. Rats can squeeze into 1-inch (2.5-cm) spaces and jump several feet in the air. These super-abilities allow them to thrive in the infinite maze of subway tunnels, sewage pipes, and concrete crannies. On trash nights, it is not uncommon to see—and hear—rats using mountains of bagged garbage as their personal playground. Recently, a New York City rat even went viral. The aptly named Pizza Rat was caught on camera hauling a slice up the subway station steps!

RELENTLESS ROACHES

Cockroaches and New York City are a tale as old as time. These pests are found in urban areas everywhere, but roaches have an unshakable association with apartment buildings in the Big Apple. Surprisingly, only the German and American roach are commonly found here, but sometimes a rare species will cause an uproar—like when scientists scrambled to identify a new critter found on the High Line. It was the first Japanese roach found in NYC!

Roaches are as ancient as dinosaurs.

Fast Facts

Number of roach species worldwide: **more than 1,000**

NYC households that have reported roaches: **30 percent**

Average lifespan of an adult roach: **400 days**

PESKY, BUT PRETTY

The latest newcomer to the NYC pest game is the spotted lanternfly. Don't let its spotted wings and bright red coloring charm you—the invasive species is wreaking havoc on trees and plants. By laying eggs on stone, metal, and a variety of city-friendly materials, populations have skyrocketed. In the spring and summer, hundreds cling to windows or cluster on sidewalks. While causing harm to wildlife is usually strictly prohibited in NYC, New Yorkers have been instructed to squish these insects on sight.

GOING GREEN

IMAGE: People taking a break by some playgrounds in Central Park.

THE PARK AT THE HEART

Central Park is New York City's most famous green space. This sanctuary in the city is home to more than 18,000 trees with an important job to do: they help cool and clean the city air by absorbing tons of carbon dioxide. Today, many wild animals call Central Park home, including raccoons, swans, ducks, and squirrels—and of course there are rats!

With numerous bodies of water, Central Park is the perfect place to hop on a boat or watch a cascading waterfall. There are also wide-open meadows for picnics, lush green spots to explore, and rocky outcrops to climb. There's no shortage of stuff to do—Central Park is a never-ending choose-your-own-adventure of fun!

IMAGE: *An aerial view of Central Park, the Upper West Side, and the Hudson River.*

Let's Rock!

In the southwest corner of Central Park sits the huge Umpire Rock—a climbing hotspot. Known as an outcrop, this rock, and the rest of Manhattan, was formed more than 500 million years ago. The grooves on the rock's surface are scars left by a glacier moving across it roughly 30,000 years ago! Summit Rock is another cool climbing spot and the highest point in the park, followed by Vista Rock, where you can visit Belvedere Castle.

Central Park is larger than the European country of Monaco. It is NYC's fifth-largest park.

ISLAND TIME

GO TO GOVERNORS

The New York mega playground of **Governors Island** is only a ten-minute ferry ride away from Manhattan—and no cars are allowed! Make the most of your visit by taking a bike ride, going wild on hilly play lawns, or lounging in the Hammock Grove (a forest grown for hammocks). The island has giant swings and NYC's longest slide! This place wasn't always so playful—keep your eyes peeled for the former military buildings rising up between green groves and ice-cream stands. History buffs can explore rich sites like Fort Jay and Castle Williams on their own or with a guided tour.

SMALL BUT MIGHTY

The adorably named **Little Island** is a newcomer to New York City, open since 2021. This tiny public park is an artificial island connected to Manhattan's Pier 54 by a short bridge. Though it is just a few steps from Hudson River Park, touching ground on Little Island transports you to a small universe hoisted into the air by towering piles that rise from the river below. The mushroom-like structures and rolling green lawns are like scenes from the pages of a Dr. Seuss book! You'll find optical illusion discs, giant instruments to jump on, and spinning chairs for play. Everything is brightly illuminated at night. During summer, enjoy concerts, arts-and-crafts events, and storytelling every day.

IMAGES: The shores of Governors Island (above); Little Island rising from the Hudson River (left).

FLOWER POWER

Towering in Queens, the 134-foot-tall (41 m) Alley Pond Giant is probably the oldest living tree in NYC, at an estimated 350 years old.

GORGEOUS GARDENS

The tallest tree at the **New York Botanical Garden** in the Bronx is 160 feet (49 m). That's about as high as a building's 15th floor! Here, you can sniff the Herb Garden's spicy bouquets and even munch on veggies at the Edible Academy. **Brooklyn Botanic Garden's** pink cherry trees are the oldest plants in the garden. They were planted in 1941 and still bloom every spring. At the **Queens Botanical Garden,** check out the buzzing honeybees at the Bee Garden—there are about 80,000! You can even adopt a honeybee to help support and protect them.

DELIGHTFUL BLOOMS

Brooklyn's **Prospect Park** took 30 years to design and build. The wait paid off: the park's indigenous forests, flowering beds, wetlands, and walking trails are a top spot for botanic-minded Brooklynites. In spring and summer, blooming buds like cherry trees, daffodils, sumac, witch hazel, and white silverbells add brilliant displays of color to every hike. Gnarled elms and dense woods turn cold-weather walks into fairy-tale jaunts. Grab a snack or picnic supplies at the plaza's bustling Greenmarket. If you want a break from hiking, check out the zoo and ice and skating rink.

> Prospect Park is home to much of Brooklyn's last remaining forests.

IMAGES: Lilies blooming in the Botanical Garden in the Bronx (above); a tranquil waterfall and wooden bridge in Prospect Park (left).

OFF THE BEATEN PATH

Fast Facts

Weight of garbage produced by NYC daily: **12,000 tons (10,900 mt)**

Weight of household waste in landfill: **150 million tons (136 million mt)**

FROM TRASH TO TREASURE

Freshkills Park, located on Staten Island, was once the largest landfill in the world! Imagine heaping waste mounds swarming with gulls. It received its last batch of trash in 2001 and today, its 2,200 acres (890 ha) are being converted into New York City's largest park. Freshkills is continuing to be rewilded—but the former trash mountain is already a haven for hikers, kayakers, and wildlife. It's also a living laboratory for scientists, who keep track of the land, water, and air quality. At Freshkills Park, nature has made a beautiful comeback.

IMAGES: A view of Manhattan from Freshkills Park (above),
the Elevated Acre on a sunny day in Manhattan (opposite top),
a tree swallow at Jamaica Bay Wildlife Refuge (opposite bottom)

SECRET GARDEN

A park in the sky? Yes! The **Elevated Acre** isn't really *off* the beaten path, but it is *up* a hidden path. This green space is high above the streets of the Financial District and between two skyscrapers! At the sanctuary on Water Street, enjoy amazing views of the Hudson River and Brooklyn Bridge. And at night, see the 50 foot (15 m) light sculpture light up the dark. Summer here brings movies under the stars!

FLOCK TO IT

This refuge is for the birds! Just a short hop, skip, and jump away from JFK Airport is one of the best birding spots in the entire Northeast—and one of the largest! At **Jamaica Bay Wildlife Refuge**, over 300 bird species have been sighted flitting, flying, and nesting among the salt marshes and tree-lined trails. Oystercatchers and yellowlegs dip their beaks into the brackish waters in spring and summer. But waterfowl are the stars of the glorious nature show, especially those that spend the winter here: snow geese show up 700 at a time!

FUN AT THE FARM

MEET THE MAKERS

New York City's **Greenmarkets** hold rainbow arrays of fruits and vegetables, as well as other foods and handmade products. While not every apple, tomato, or potato at the more than 50 open-air markets comes from the five boroughs, everything is local to the Northeast. Sample honey from Pennsylvania or crisp cider from Upstate New York. Smell lavender flowers grown in New Jersey. Find a fish from the New York coastline or a funky mushroom sprouted in the Catskill Mountains. The rows of white-topped tents, bountiful tables, and sizzling sample stations are guaranteed to tingle your taste buds.

RAISE THE ROOF(TOP)

New York City is always buzzing with activity, even on the roof! **Brooklyn Grange** is the most abundant green rooftop in the boroughs. It operates three of the world's largest rooftop soil farms, right in the city. Sustainable urban living is the name of the game—people grow and sell honey, varieties of vegetables, and even homemade hot sauce. Here, visitors can dig in and plant soil beds and harvest greens. To keep it all growing, Brooklyn Grange uses a whopping 1.2 million pounds (544,300 kg) of soil!

IMAGES: Shoppers browse fruits and vegetables at a Greenmarket (above); a top-down view of Brooklyn Grange (left).

SECRETS OF THE CITY

IMAGE: Belvedere Castle overlooking Turtle Pond.

SEARCH CENTRAL PARK

Birders in the Ramble can record their sightings in a logbook at the Central Park Boathouse.

RAMBLE ON

Escape the city—without leaving the city—in the **Ramble**. Entering this magical woodland feels like wandering into a fairy tale. The 36-acre (14-ha) tree-filled wonderland was designed to mimic the lush forests of Upstate New York with a heavy sprinkling of twisting paths, streams, winding trails, natural bridges, and rocks. Find the blooming shrubs of Azalea Pond or the Stone Arch before resting at the rustic Summerhouse. Ramblers often get lost in this secret garden, so don't forget your map—or your binoculars!

IMAGES: The Ramble Stone Arch (above); Belvedere Castle (opposite top); Alice in Wonderland *sculpture (opposite bottom).*

EXPLORE A CASTLE

A castle in the city! **Belvedere Castle** is one of Central Park's most famous features, and it's easy to see why: this "miniature" castle boasts a regal tower, stone terrace, and rising pavilions. It was built out of Manhattan schist rock dug up from Central Park and was once a weather station! Today, the castle still holds equipment that measures temperature, wind, and rainfall. Look for the broze cockatrice. This mythical combination of a dragon, snake, and rooster lurks above one of the castle's doorways.

Fast Facts

Location: **East 74th Street, just north of the Conservatory Water**

Height: **9.6 feet (3 m)**

Width: **14.5 feet (4.4 m)**

WORLD OF WONDER

A huge bronze sculpture called *Alice in Wonderland* brings Alice and her friends to life in Central Park. Alice sits with her cat, Dinah, and Doormouse, the Cheshire Cat, Mad Hatter, and White Rabbit. Here, it's okay to touch the art—and even climb it! The top of the giant mushroom has plenty of space to take a seat. Underneath is the perfect place for a shady seat on a hot, sunny day. Over the years, so many kids have climbed and crawled on the statue that they have smoothed and polished it!

GO UNDERGROUND

SUBWAY SONGS

If you're waiting on the N/Q/R/W platforms at 34th Street, you might hear strange sounds ringing through the station between the whoosh of passing trains. Its source is a green tube-like structure above your head—a giant instrument hidden in plain sight! It's called *Reach: New York*. Wave your hands in front of the tube's small holes and you might hear sounds ranging from xylophone notes to frog croaks.

The sounds in the giant *Reach: New York* instrument are updated every year.

MOVIE ON THE MOVE

Want to catch a movie on the train? Hop on a Manhattan-bound B or Q at Dekalb Avenue in Brooklyn for a front-row seat to *Masstransiscope*. This painted image installed on the subway tunnel wall uses reflective material, fluorescent lights, and an enclosure designed to bring optical science and art to life. As you ride by, the bright geometric shapes move like images in a flip-book. Don't blink: it only lasts 20 seconds!

IMAGES: An entrance to the 34th Street subway station (above); the Q train above ground (left); one of several *Life Underground* sculptures (opposite top); bars of gold (opposite bottom).

SCAVENGE THE STATION

Have a scavenger hunt while waiting for your A, C, E, or L trains at 14th Street by searching for the *Life Underground* sculptures. Can you find an elephant in heels? A sewer alligator trying to chow down on a man whose head is a bag of money? Bulbous Metropolitan Transportation Authority workers hanging off a steel girder or sweeping up old-fashioned subway tokens? These small bronze statues are not only adorable, but they also playfully capture New York City legends—and some of the city's most notable characters.

After an alligator was discovered in a Harlem sewer, February 9 was declared Alligator in the Sewer Day in NYC.

BURIED TREASURE

Deep below the Federal Reserve Bank of New York Building, a massive vault is carved into Manhattan bedrock. The secret compartment is filled with gold! The **Federal Reserve Gold Vault** is highly secure. Its one entry is protected by a 90-ton (81-mt), 9-foot-tall (3 m) steel cylinder within a 140-ton (127-mt) frame. The gold belongs to the governments of various countries, including the US. For security, at least three people must be present whenever the gold is moved—even to clean or change a light bulb!

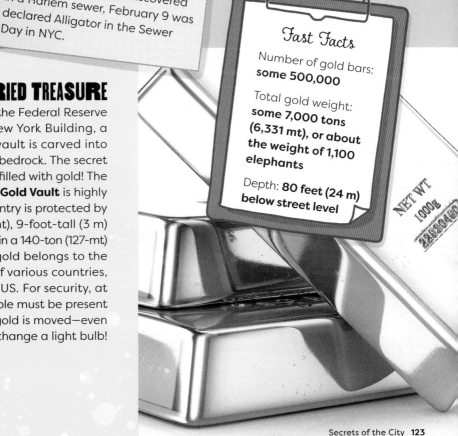

Fast Facts

Number of gold bars: **some 500,000**

Total gold weight: **some 7,000 tons (6,331 mt), or about the weight of 1,100 elephants**

Depth: **80 feet (24 m) below street level**

BEST-KEPT SECRETS

Magician Harry Houdini's bathtub is on display inside the shop.

MAKE SOME MAGIC

Behold: America's oldest magic store! Tucked away on the sixth floor of an unadorned building on West 34th Street in Manhattan is **Tannen's Magic Shop**, a walkable maze of every trick of the trade imaginable, from puzzle coins to silk scarves to actual crystal balls. If you're serious about becoming a master magician, Tannen's hosts a weeklong magic camp with clandestine classes from the world's greatest magicians! They teach the tricks and techniques of the trade. (Note: the camp is hosted in Pennsylvania to avoid prying eyes.)

IMAGES: A magician demonstrates a card trick (above); a glimpse inside Inwood Hill Park (opposite top); a one-acre (0.4-ha) farm in Manhattan (opposite bottom).

ANCIENT CAVES

In 1895, secret caves were discovered at what is now **Inwood Hill Park** in northern Manhattan. The caves were once used as a place for food storage and as shelter during extreme weather by the Lenape Native Americans who lived here. How do we know? Pottery, fireplaces, and even preserved foods under ash were found in the caves! Tools and weapons like axes were also found in the area. Today, the site is an archaeological treasure.

SECRET (MINI) GARDENS

If you're walking the streets of New York, chances are you're not far from a community garden—there are more than 550 in the city! But these green gems are easy to miss—many are as tiny as a few steps across. Others are larger, like **El Sitio Feliz** in Harlem. This garden is 20,000 square feet (1,858 sq m), the size of eight back-to-back tennis courts! Many gardens were once abandoned lots. Volunteers transformed them into thriving spaces for gathering and for growing food. Even better—much of the food is donated to people in need.

HUNT FOR HIDDEN GEMS

JUST A WHISPER

If you see someone facing a corner in Grand Central Terminal's lower floor, they're probably using the hidden **Whispering Gallery**. The magnificent tiled arches create an acoustic magic trick: if two people whisper into opposite corners, they'll be able to hear each other from across the vaulted hall as if they were standing next to each other! Grab a friend or family member and try it out.

The founder of the New York Herald wanted to be buried in a 200-foot-tall (61 m) tomb in the shape of an owl.

EERIE EYES

Night owls should head to the north side of **Herald Square** after dusk. Look for the two bronze owls with green glowing eyes perched on top of a tall monument. These eerie prowlers once adorned the building that was home to the old New York Herald newspaper, whose founder was fond of these feathered friends. The green orbs have been blinking for more than 100 years. Most New Yorkers walk right by this eerie art without a second glance.

PERFECT POPS

6½ Avenue is a secret street hidden between Sixth and Seventh Avenues and the only street in NYC with a fractioned number. It runs from West 57th to West 51st Street, and no cars are allowed. Entering this petite passageway is like finding a secret shortcut into an entirely new place. Here, you can enjoy a bite as you make your way along. And if it's raining, it's the perfect place to take shelter—most of the avenue is covered! There are over 500 similar secret spaces hidden all over the city, and each is its own buried treasure.

WHERE'S THE WIZARD?

New York is the Big Apple, but its riches come in every size. The **Wizard of Park Avenue** is one of its tinier treasures. The robed sorcerer can be seen casting a spell over 32nd Street and Park Avenue, waving his wand from a clock throne. The cast-iron timepiece sits on a building that once housed a silk importer. Look closely to find the cocoon and moth carvings. The "Silk Clock," crafted in 1926, is only one of NYC's many small wonders.

IMAGES: 6½ Avenue (above); a side view of the Wizard of Park Avenue (right); the iconic Oyster Bar & Restaurant within Grand Central Terminal (opposite top); a bronze owl in Herald Square (opposite bottom).

TAKE THE THRONE

LUXURY LOO

Finding a bathroom in the Big Apple can be hit or miss. But if you've gotta go, there's no more luxurious place than the public restroom in **Bryant Park**. In peak seaon, this bathroom receives upward of 3,000 flushes in one day! Here, your ceramic throne is surrounded by natural light from tall, frosted windows and has fresh flowers, gorgeous artwork, and a bathroom attendant. The sounds of tinkling and handwashing are accompanied by subtle classical music piped in through speakers.

Fast Facts

Year constructed: **1869**

Average water used per flush: **3 to 6 ounces (89 to 177 ml)**

Water saved per year: **250,000 gallons (946,300 L)**

WELL, WELL, WELL

Another historic toilet can be found in Prospect Park. **The Wellhouse** is one of the park's oldest structures, originally constructed by Prospect's first designers and *park*-itects. It was recently restyled with a modern twist and made into the city's first compostable public restroom! Not only do these toilets turn waste into compost—with the help of thousands of worms—its water is recycled into greywater, which helps irrigate the park. An underground platform allows visitors to marvel at the Wellhouse's mechanics.

IMAGES: The luxurious bathroom at Bryant Park (above); the Wellhouse on a snowy day (left).

WHAT'S THE DIFFERENCE?

Times Square is one busy place! Can you spot the five differences between these two pictures? See answers on page 140.

WHAT'S THE DIFFERENCE?

Lady Liberty is a sight to behold! Can you spot the five differences between these two pictures? See answers on page 140.

INDEX

RESOURCES & PHOTO CREDITS

Getting Around Town (pages 20-31)
Central Park Boathouse: centralparkboathouse.com
Metropolitan Transportation Authority (MTA): new.mta.info
MTA Bus Time: bustime.mta.info
NYC Ferry: ferry.nyc
Roosevelt Island Tram: rioc.ny.gov
Staten Island Ferry: siferry.com
The High Line: thehighline.org
Transit Museum: nytransitmuseum.org

Places to Play (pages 32-45)
Brooklyn Children's Museum: brooklynkids.org
Brooklyn Nets: nba.com/nets
Coney Island Official: coneyisland.com
Deno's Wonder Wheel & Amusement Park: denoswonderwheel.com
Intrepid Museum: intrepidmuseum.org
Jacob Riis Beach: riisbeach.nyc
Luna Park Official: lunaparknyc.com
New York Hall of Science: nysci.org
US Open: usopen.org
Yankee Stadium: mlb.com/yankees

What a View! (pages 46-57)
American Museum of Natural History: amnh.org
Brooklyn Bridge Park: brooklynbridgepark.org
Ellis Island & Statue of Liberty: statueofliberty.org
Empire State Building: esbnyc.com
Grand Central: grandcentralterminal.com
Metropolitan Museum: metmuseum.org
New York Public Library: nypl.org
Rockefeller Center: rockefellercenter.com
One World Observatory: oneworldobservatory.com

Let's Eat! (pages 58-69)
Chinatown Ice Cream Factory: chinatownicecreamfactory.com
Economy Candy: economycandy.com
Essex Market: essexmarket.nyc
Junior's: juniorscheesecake.com
Katz's Delicatessen: katzsdelicatessen.com
Lombardi's: firstpizza.com
Magnolia Bakery: magnoliabakery.com
Nathan's Famous: nathansfamous.com
Nom Wah: nomwah.com
Queens Night Market: queensnightmarket.com
Russ & Daughters: russanddaughters.com
Serendipity 3: serendipity3.com
Smorgasburg: smorgasburg.com
Street Vendor Project: streetvendor.org
Sylvia's: sylviasrestaurant.com
Veniero's: venieros.com
Zabar's: zabars.com

Heading to Broadway (pages 70-81)
Broadway Shows: broadway.com
Broadway Theater District: broadwaytheaterdistrict.com
Macy's: macys.com
Museum of Broadway: themuseumofbroadway.com
Museum of the Moving Image: movingimage.org
Teatro SEA: teatrosea.org
Times Square: timessquarenyc.org
Trinity Church: trinitywallstreet.org

IMAGE CREDITS
Illustrations © 2025 John Foster
8-9: Predrag Vuckovic/Getty Images / **12-13:** Tetra images/Getty Images / **13:** Alexander Spatari/Getty Images / **14:** Bokic Bojan/Shutterstock (Empire State Building); Fresh photos from all over the world/Getty Images (Broadway); Matteo Colombo/Getty Images (bridge); © Guillaume Gaudet/Lonely Planet (Flatiron) / **15:** Gowri Vallaban Panneer Selvam/Getty Images (tiger); Pierre E. Debbas/Shutterstock (stadium); dszc/Getty Images (Central Park) / **16:** Alon Adika/Shutterstock / **18:** Image Source/Steve Prezant/Getty Images / **19:** CHNT/Shutterstock / **20-21:** PeskyMonkey/Getty Images / **22:** nyker/Shutterstock / **23:** Diego Grandi/Shutterstock / **24:** Michael Lee/Getty Images / **25-27:** oneinchpunch/Shutterstock (Grand Central); aluxum/Getty Images (Broadway) / **26:** © Marco Bottigelli/Getty Images / **28:** © Vincent Tullo/NYC & Company / **29:** The Curious Eye/Shutterstock (sign); pisaphotography/Shutterstock (High Line Park) / **30:** agsaz/Shutterstock / **31:** rmbarricarte/Getty Images (lake); Popova Valeriya/Shutterstock (cycle rickshaw) / **32-33:** Juana Nunez/Shutterstock / **34:** Roy Rochlin/Getty Images (Domino Park Playground); Sergi Reboredo/Alamy Stock Photo (Seward Park) / **35:** Edd Westmacott/Alamy Stock Photo (slide); Robert Kneschke/Shutterstock (pirates) / **36:** Boaz Rottem/Alamy Stock Photo / **37:** Sergi Reboredo/Alamy Stock Photo (Maker Faire); EQRoy/Shutterstock (planes) / **38-39:** Ryan McVay/Getty Images / **39:** Annalisa Cimmino/Getty Images / **40:** juliahenderson/Getty Images / **41:** Here Now/Shutterstock (beach); Jamie Grill/Getty Images (surfers) / **42:** Leonard Zhukovsky/Shutterstock / **43:** ExaMedia Photography/Shutterstock / **44:** Patrick Hatt/Shutterstock (bugs); Leonard Zhukovsky/Shutterstock (horses) / **45:** Ritu Manoj Jethani/Shutterstock (fish); Martin LAW/Shutterstock (carousel) / **46-47:** Alexander Prokopenko/Shutterstock / **48:** EXTREME-PHOTOGRAPHER/Getty Images / **49:** f11photo/Shutterstock (One World); Sean Pavone/Shutterstock (Top of the Rock) / **50:** Busakorn Pongparnit/Getty Images / **51:** Steve Cukrov/Shutterstock / **52:** Lucas Alvarez Canga/Shutterstock / **53:** Jeffrey Greenberg/Universal Images Group via Getty Images / **54:** Wangkun Jia/Shutterstock / **55:** MACH Photos/Shutterstock / **56-57:** Matteo Colombo/Getty Images / **58-59:** Beverly Logan/Getty Images / **60:** Brent Hofacker/Shutterstock / **61:** DronG/Shutterstock (chicken); Michael Kraus/Shutterstock (egg cream) / **62:** BROOK PIFER/Getty Images / **63:** Liudmyla Chuhunova/Shutterstock (hot dog); pingpongcat/Shutterstock (bagel) / **64:**

Stuart Monk/Shutterstock / 65: Allen.G/Shutterstock (market); J. Lee - Jeffrey's Photos/Shutterstock (BEC sandwich) / 66: a katz/Shutterstock (hot dog contest); © Sivan Askayo/Lonely Planet (sandwich) / 67: Here Now/Shutterstock (Sylvia's); © Guillaume Gaudet/Lonely Planet (Nom Wah) / 68: Michael Data/Shutterstock / 69: Manu Padilla/Shutterstock (ice cream); Edward Westmacott/Alamy Stock Photo (candy) / 70-71: Fresh photos from all over the world/Getty Images / 72-73: Candy Kempsey/Shutterstock / 73: Susan Law Cain/Shutterstock / 74: focusstock/Getty Images / 75: SeanPavonePhoto/Getty Images (Columbus Circle); gary718/Shutterstock (panda) / 76: Rolf E. Staerk/Shutterstock / 77: travelview/Shutterstock (Cloisters); © Guillaume Gaudet/Lonely Planet (Flatiron) /78-79: Luciano Mortula - LGM/Shutterstock / 79: Nancy Ann Ellis/Shutterstock / 80: Africa Studio/Shutterstock / 81: Everett Collection/Shutterstock / 82-83: Trish Mayo/Getty Images / 84: Joe Tabacca/Shutterstock / 85: © Guillaume Gaudet/Lonely Planet / 86-87: Stock Montage/Getty Images / 88: Anthony Correia/Shutterstock / 89: agsaz/Shutterstock / 90: Christina Horsten/picture alliance via Getty Images / 91: JOHANNES EISELE/AFP via Getty Images (dog); lev radin/Shutterstock (parade) / 92: Steve Sanchez Photos/Shutterstock (parade); Mihai_Andritoiu/Shutterstock (dragon) / 93: lazyllama/Shutterstock (Pride); Dariusz Gryczka/Shutterstock (runners) / 94-95: Radomir Rezny/Shutterstock / 96: Mariusz Lopusiewicz/Shutterstock / 97: Steve Ikeguchi/Shutterstock (pigeon); Mike Stobe/Getty Images (hawk) / 98: slam Dogru/Anadolu Agency via Getty Images / 99: Little Vignettes Photo/Getty Images

/ 100-101: shu2260/Shutterstock / 102: Andrew Lichtenstein/Corbis via Getty Images / 103: rblfmr/Shutterstock (cat); Susan Watts/NY Daily News Archive via Getty Images (hawk) / 104: John A. Anderson/Shutterstock / 105: Amy Lutz/Shutterstock (lanternfly); kirill guzhvinsky/Shutterstock (roach) / 106-107: Jordi De Rueda Roigé/Alamy Stock Photo / 108-109: Bluberries/Getty Images / 110: George Wirt/Shutterstock / 111: Michael Lee/Getty Images / 112: solepsizm/Shutterstock / 113: Boogich/Getty Images / 114: Richard Levine/Alamy Stock Photo / 115: Larsek/Shutterstock (bird); Andriy Prokopenko/Getty Images (park) / 116: Gabby Jones/Bloomberg via Getty Images / 117: Little Vignettes Photo/Shutterstock / 118-119: © Stefano Giovannini/Lonely Planet / 120: Alexandre Tziripouloff/Shutterstock / 121: travelview/Shutterstock (statue); © Stefano Giovannini/Lonely Planet (castle) / 122: RonGreer. Com/Shutterstock (subway); pisaphotography/Shutterstock (sign) / 123: T photography/Shutterstock (statue); OscarDominguez/Shutterstock (gold bars) / 124: Yuganov Konstantin/Shutterstock / 125: Little Vignettes Photo/Shutterstock (garden); Barry Winiker/Getty Images (forest) / 126: Bruce Yuanyue Bi/Getty Images (monument); Little Vignettes Photo/Shutterstock (restaurant) / 127: Leonard Zhukovsky/Shutterstock (buildings); quiggyt4/Shutterstock (wizard) / 128: Roy Rochlin/Getty Images / 129: DON EMMERT/AFP via Getty Images / 130: Luciano Mortula - LGM/Shutterstock / 132: OlegAlbinsky/Getty Images / 141: Lee O/Shutterstock

WHAT'S THE DIFFERENCE? ANSWERS

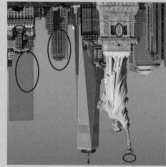

Central Park gets more than 40 million visitors each year.